MznLnx

Missing Links Exam Preps

Exam Prep for

Financial Management Principles and Applications

Keown, Martin, Petty, Scott, Jr., 10th Edition

The MznLnx Exam Prep is your link from the texbook and lecture to your exams.
The MznLnx Exam Preps are unauthorized and comprehensive reviews of your textbooks.

All material provided by MznLnx and Rico Publications (c) 2010
Textbook publishers and textbook authors do not particpate in or contribute to these reviews.

MznLnx

Rico Publications

Exam Prep for Financial Management Principles and Applications
10th Edition
Keown, Martin, Petty, Scott, Jr.

Publisher: Raymond Houge
Assistant Editor: Michael Rouger
Text and Cover Designer: Lisa Buckner
Marketing Manager: Sara Swagger
Project Manager, Editorial Production: Jerry Emerson
Art Director: Vernon Lowerui

Product Manager: Dave Mason
Editorial Assitant: Rachel Guzmanji
Pedagogy: Debra Long
Cover Image: Jim Reed/Getty Images
Text and Cover Printer: City Printing, Inc.
Compositor: Media Mix, Inc.

(c) 2010 Rico Publications

ALL RIGHTS RESERVED. No part of this work covered by the copyright may be reproduced or used in any form or by an means--graphic, electronic, or mechanical, including photocopying, recording, taping, Web distribution, information storage, and retrieval systems, or in any other manner--without the written permission of the publisher.

Printed in the United States
ISBN:

For more information about our products, contact us at:
Dave.Mason@RicoPublications.com

For permission to use material from this text or product, submit a request online to:
Dave.Mason@RicoPublications.com

Contents

CHAPTER 1
An Introduction to Financial Management — 1

CHAPTER 2
Understanding Financial Statements, Taxes, and Cash Flows — 13

CHAPTER 3
Evaluating a Firm's Financial Performance — 24

CHAPTER 4
Financial Forecasting, Planning, and Budgeting — 32

CHAPTER 5
The Value of Money — 37

CHAPTER 6
Risk and Rates of Return — 42

CHAPTER 7
Valuation and Characteristics of Bonds — 49

CHAPTER 8
Stock Valuation — 56

CHAPTER 9
Capital Budgeting Decision Criteria — 62

CHAPTER 10
Cash Flows and Other Topics in Capital Budgeting — 66

CHAPTER 11
Capital Budgeting and Risk Analysis — 72

CHAPTER 12
Cost of Capital — 77

CHAPTER 13
Managing for Shareholder Value — 86

CHAPTER 14
The Role of Financial Markets in Financial Management — 92

CHAPTER 15
Analysis and Impact of Leverage — 101

CHAPTER 16
Planning the Firm's Financing Mix — 106

CHAPTER 17
Dividend Policy and Internal Financing — 117

CHAPTER 18
Working-Capital Management and Short-Term Financing — 122

CHAPTER 19
Cash and Marketable Securities Management — 129

CHAPTER 20
Accounts Receivable and Inventory Management — 135

Contents (Cont.)

CHAPTER 21
  Risk Management — 138
CHAPTER 22
  International Business Finance — 147
ANSWER KEY — 153

TO THE STUDENT

COMPREHENSIVE

The *MznLnx* Exam Prep series is designed to help you pass your exams. Editors at MznLnx review your textbooks and then prepare these practice exams to help you master the textbook material. Unlike study guides, workbooks, and practice tests provided by the texbook publisher and textbook authors, *MznLnx* gives you **all** of the material in each chapter in exam form, not just samples, so you can be sure to nail your exam.

MECHANICAL

The MznLnx Exam Prep series creates exams that will help you learn the subject matter as well as test you on your understanding. Each question is designed to help you master the concept. Just working through the exams, you gain an understanding of the subject--its a simple mechanical process that produces success.

INTEGRATED STUDY GUIDE AND REVIEW

MznLnx is not just a set of exams designed to test you, its also a comprehensive review of the subject content. Each exam question is also a review of the concept, making sure that you will get the answer correct without having to go to other sources of material. You learn as you go! Its the easiest way to pass an exam.

HUMOR

Studying can be tedious and dry. MznLnx's instructional design includes moderate humor within the exam questions on occassion, to break the tedium and revitalize the brain

Chapter 1. An Introduction to Financial Management

1. _____ is the difference between price and the costs of bringing to market whatever it is that is accounted as an enterprise (whether by harvest, extraction, manufacture, or purchase) in terms of the component costs of delivered goods and/or services and any operating or other expenses.

A key difficulty in measuring profit is in defining costs. Pure economic monetary profits can be zero or negative even in competitive equilibrium when accounted monetized costs exceed monetized price.

    a. Economic profit
    b. A Random Walk Down Wall Street
    c. AAB
    d. Accounting profit

2. In economics, _____ is the process by which a firm determines the price and output level that returns the greatest profit. There are several approaches to this problem. The total revenue--total cost method relies on the fact that profit equals revenue minus cost, and the marginal revenue--marginal cost method is based on the fact that total profit in a perfectly competitive market reaches its maximum point where marginal revenue equals marginal cost.

    a. Net profit margin
    b. 4-4-5 Calendar
    c. Profit maximization
    d. Profit margin

3. In the commercial and legal parlance of most countries, a _____ or simply a partnership, refers to an association of persons or an unincorporated company with the following major features:

- Created by agreement, proof of existence and estoppel.
- Formed by two or more persons
- The owners are all personally liable for any legal actions and debts the company may face

It is a partnership in which partners share equally in both responsibility and liability.

Partnerships have certain default characteristics relating to both the relationship between the individual partners and (b) the relationship between the partnership and the outside world. The former can generally be overridden by agreement between the partners, whereas the latter generally cannot be.

The assets of the business are owned on behalf of the other partners, and they are each personally liable, jointly and severally, for business debts, taxes or tortious liability.

    a. Federal Home Loan Mortgage Corporation
    b. First Prudential Markets
    c. The Depository Trust ' Clearing Corporation
    d. General partnership

4. A _____ is a form of partnership similar to a general partnership, except that in addition to one or more general partners (GPs), there are one or more limited partners (_____s). It is a partnership in which only one partner is required to be a general partner.

The GPs are, in all major respects, in the same legal position as partners in a conventional firm, i.e. they have management control, share the right to use partnership property, share the profits of the firm in predefined proportions, and have joint and several liability for the debts of the partnership.

    a. Limited partnership
    b. Limited liability company
    c. Fund of funds
    d. Leverage

5. A _____ is a type of business entity in which partners (owners) share with each other the profits or losses of the business undertaking in which all have invested. _____s are often favored over corporations for taxation purposes, as the _____ structure does not generally incur a tax on profits before it is distributed to the partners (i.e. there is no dividend tax levied.) However, depending on the _____ structure and the jurisdiction in which it operates, owners of a _____ may be exposed to greater personal liability than they would as shareholders of a corporation.
   a. Clayton Antitrust Act   b. National Securities Markets Improvement Act of 1996
   c. Fiduciary   d. Partnership

6. A sole _____, or simply _____ is a type of business entity which legally has no separate existence from its owner. Hence, the limitations of liability enjoyed by a corporation and limited liability partnerships do not apply to sole proprietors. All debts of the business are debts of the owner.
   a. Product life cycle   b. Just-in-time
   c. Free cash flow   d. Proprietorship

7. The institution most often referenced by the word '_____' is a public or publicly traded _____, the shares of which are traded on a public stock exchange (e.g., the New York Stock Exchange or Nasdaq in the United States) where shares of stock of _____s are bought and sold by and to the general public. Most of the largest businesses in the world are publicly traded _____s. However, the majority of _____s are said to be closely held, privately held or close _____s, meaning that no ready market exists for the trading of shares.
   a. Depository Trust Company   b. Federal Home Loan Mortgage Corporation
   c. Protect   d. Corporation

8. _____ is a concept whereby a person's financial liability is limited to a fixed sum, most commonly the value of a person's investment in a company or partnership with _____. A shareholder in a limited company is not personally liable for any of the debts of the company, other than for the value of his investment in that company. The same is true for the members of a _____ partnership and the limited partners in a limited partnership.
   a. Personal property   b. Sarbanes-Oxley Act
   c. Beneficial owner   d. Limited liability

9. A _____ in the law of the vast majority of United States jurisdictions is a legal form of business company that provides limited liability to its owners. It is a hybrid business entity having certain characteristics of both a corporation and a partnership or sole proprietorship (depending on how many owners there are.) The primary characteristic an _____ shares with a corporation is limited liability, and the primary characteristic it shares with a partnership is the availability of pass-through income taxation.
   a. Fund of funds   b. Financial endowment
   c. Pension fund   d. Limited liability company

10. In the most general sense, a _____ is anything that is a hindrance, or puts individuals at a disadvantage.

Before we discuss the financial terms, we should note that a _____ can also have a much more important slang meaning.

This is best described in an example.

a. McFadden Act
b. Limited liability
c. Liability
d. Covenant

11. In economics, a _____ is a mechanism that allows people to easily buy and sell (trade) financial securities (such as stocks and bonds), commodities (such as precious metals or agricultural goods), and other fungible items of value at low transaction costs and at prices that reflect the efficient-market hypothesis.

_____s have evolved significantly over several hundred years and are undergoing constant innovation to improve liquidity.

Both general markets (where many commodities are traded) and specialized markets (where only one commodity is traded) exist.

a. Secondary market
b. Cost of carry
c. Delta hedging
d. Financial market

12. _____, is when a company issues common stock or shares to the public for the first time. They are often issued by smaller, younger companies seeking capital to expand, but can also be done by large privately-owned companies looking to become publicly traded.

In an _____ the issuer may obtain the assistance of an underwriting firm, which helps it determine what type of security to issue (common or preferred), best offering price and time to bring it to market.

a. Insolvency
b. Asian Financial Crisis
c. Initial public offering
d. Interest

13. The _____ is that part of the capital markets that deals with the issuance of new securities. Companies, governments or public sector institutions can obtain funding through the sale of a new stock or bond issue. This is typically done through a syndicate of securities dealers.

a. Primary market
b. Peer group analysis
c. Volatility clustering
d. Sector rotation

14. The _____ is the financial market where previously issued securities and financial instruments such as stock, bonds, options, and futures are bought and sold. The term '_____' is also used refer to the market for any used goods or assets, or an alternative use for an existing product or asset where the customer base is the second market

With primary issuances of securities or financial instruments, or the primary market, investors purchase these securities directly from issuers such as corporations issuing shares in an IPO or private placement, or directly from the federal government in the case of treasuries.

a. Delta neutral
b. Financial market
c. Secondary market
d. Performance attribution

15. A _____ is a situation that involves losing one quality or aspect of something in return for gaining another quality or aspect. It implies a decision to be made with full comprehension of both the upside and downside of a particular choice.

In economics the term is expressed as opportunity cost, referring the most preferred alternative given up.

a. Capital outflow
c. Break-even point
b. Total revenue
d. Trade-off

16. _____ is the balance of the amounts of cash being received and paid by a business during a defined period of time, sometimes tied to a specific project. Measurement of _____ can be used

- to evaluate the state or performance of a business or project.
- to determine problems with liquidity. Being profitable does not necessarily mean being liquid. A company can fail because of a shortage of cash, even while profitable.
- to generate project rate of returns. The time of _____s into and out of projects are used as inputs to financial models such as internal rate of return, and net present value.
- to examine income or growth of a business when it is believed that accrual accounting concepts do not represent economic realities. Alternately, _____ can be used to 'validate' the net income generated by accrual accounting.

_____ as a generic term may be used differently depending on context, and certain _____ definitions may be adapted by analysts and users for their own uses. Common terms include operating _____ and free _____.

_____s can be classified into:

1. Operational _____s: Cash received or expended as a result of the company's core business activities.
2. Investment _____s: Cash received or expended through capital expenditure, investments or acquisitions.
3. Financing _____s: Cash received or expended as a result of financial activities, such as interests and dividends.

All three together - the net _____ - are necessary to reconcile the beginning cash balance to the ending cash balance. Loan draw downs or equity injections, that is just shifting of capital but no expenditure as such, are not considered in the net _____.

a. Shareholder value
c. Cash flow
b. Corporate finance
d. Real option

17. In financial accounting, a _____ or statement of cash flows is a financial statement that shows a company's flow of cash. The money coming into the business is called cash inflow, and money going out from the business is called cash outflow. The statement shows how changes in balance sheet and income accounts affect cash and cash equivalents, and breaks the analysis down to operating, investing, and financing activities.

a. 7-Eleven
c. 529 plan
b. 4-4-5 Calendar
d. Cash flow statement

Chapter 1. An Introduction to Financial Management 5

18. '_____' is a cliched expression sometimes used in analyzing businesses; it refers to the importance of cash flow in the overall fiscal health of the business. The phrase is a favorite of Alex Spanos and has sometimes appeared in Motley Fool articles and commentaries. It describes the importance of sufficient cash as an asset in the business for short term operations, purchases and acquisitions.
  a. Corporate finance
  b. Cash flow
  c. Rights issue
  d. Cash is king

19. In finance, the value of an option consists of two components, its intrinsic value and its _____. Time value is simply the difference between option value and intrinsic value. _____ is also known as theta, extrinsic value, or instrumental value.
  a. Debt buyer
  b. Global Squeeze
  c. Conservatism
  d. Time value

20. Simply put, _____ is the value of money figuring in a given amount of interest for a given amount of time. For example 100 dollars of todays money held for a year at 5 percent interest is worth 105 dollars, therefore 100 dollars paid now or 105 dollars paid exactly one year from now is the same amount of payment of money with that given intersest at that given amount of time. This notion dates at least to Martín de Azpilcueta of the School of Salamanca.

All of the standard calculations for _____ derive from the most basic algebraic expression for the present value of a future sum, 'discounted' to the present by an amount equal to the _____. For example, a sum of FV to be received in one year is discounted (at the rate of interest r) to give a sum of PV at present: PV = FV -- rÂ·PV = FV/(1+r).

  a. Current account
  b. Coefficient of variation
  c. Zero-coupon bond
  d. Time value of money

21. _____ measures the nominal future sum of money that a given sum of money is 'worth' at a specified time in the future assuming a certain interest rate rate of return; it is the present value multiplied by the accumulation function.

The value does not include corrections for inflation or other factors that affect the true value of money in the future. This is used in time value of money calculations.

  a. Discounted cash flow
  b. Future-oriented
  c. Present value of costs
  d. Future value

22. _____ is the planning process used to determine whether a firm's long term investments such as new machinery, replacement machinery, new plants, new products, and research development projects are worth pursuing. It is budget for major capital, or investment, expenditures.

Many formal methods are used in _____, including the techniques such as

- Net present value
- Profitability index
- Internal rate of return
- Modified Internal Rate of Return
- Equivalent annuity

These methods use the incremental cash flows from each potential investment, or project. Techniques based on accounting earnings and accounting rules are sometimes used - though economists consider this to be improper - such as the accounting rate of return, and 'return on investment.' Simplified and hybrid methods are used as well, such as payback period and discounted payback period.

a. Preferred stock
c. Shareholder value
b. Financial distress
d. Capital budgeting

23. In economics, business, and accounting, a _____ is the value of money that has been used up to produce something, and hence is not available for use anymore. In business, the _____ may be one of acquisition, in which case the amount of money expended to acquire it is counted as _____. In this case, money is the input that is gone in order to acquire the thing.

a. Marginal cost
c. Cost
b. Sliding scale fees
d. Fixed costs

24. _____, in microeconomics, are the cost advantages that a business obtains due to expansion. _____ may be utilized by any size firm expanding its scale of operation.

a. Economies of scale
c. Articles of incorporation
b. Employee Retirement Income Security Act
d. Uniform Commercial Code

25. In marketing, _____ is the process of distinguishing the differences of a product or offering from others, to make it more attractive to a particular target market. This involves differentiating it from competitors' products as well as one's own product offerings.

_____ is a source of competitive advantage. Although research in a niche market may result in changing your product in order to improve differentiation, the changes themselves are not differentiation.

a. 4-4-5 Calendar
c. 7-Eleven
b. 529 plan
d. Product differentiation

26. The _____ is the market for securities, where companies and governments can raise longterm funds. The _____ includes the stock market and the bond market. Financial regulators, such as the U.S. Securities and Exchange Commission, oversee the _____s in their designated countries to ensure that investors are protected against fraud.

a. Spot rate
c. Forward market
b. Capital market
d. Delta neutral

27. In political science and economics, the _____ or agency dilemma treats the difficulties that arise under conditions of incomplete and asymmetric information when a principal hires an agent. Various mechanisms may be used to try to align the interests of the agent with those of the principal, such as piece rates/commissions, profit sharing, efficiency wages, performance measurement (including financial statements), the agent posting a bond, or fear of firing. The _____ is found in most employer/employee relationships, for example, when stockholders hire top executives of corporations.
   a. Principal-agent problem
   b. 4-4-5 Calendar
   c. 7-Eleven
   d. 529 plan

28. _____ in finance is a risk management technique, related to hedging, that mixes a wide variety of investments within a portfolio. Because the fluctuations of a single security have less impact on a diverse portfolio, _____ minimizes the risk from any one investment.

A simple example of _____ is the following: On a particular island the entire economy consists of two companies: one that sells umbrellas and another that sells sunscreen.

   a. 4-4-5 Calendar
   b. 7-Eleven
   c. Diversification
   d. 529 plan

29. In business and accounting, _____s are everything of value that is owned by a person or company. The balance sheet of a firm records the monetary value of the _____s owned by the firm. The two major _____ classes are tangible _____s and intangible _____s.
   a. Income
   b. Accounts payable
   c. EBITDA
   d. Asset

30. In economic models, the _____ time frame assumes no fixed factors of production. Firms can enter or leave the marketplace, and the cost (and availability) of land, labor, raw materials, and capital goods can be assumed to vary. In contrast, in the short-run time frame, certain factors are assumed to be fixed, because there is not sufficient time for them to change.
   a. Short-run
   b. 4-4-5 Calendar
   c. 529 plan
   d. Long-run

31. _____ is the set of processes, customs, policies, laws and institutions affecting the way a corporation is directed, administered or controlled. _____ also includes the relationships among the many stakeholders involved and the goals for which the corporation is governed. The principal stakeholders are the shareholders, management and the board of directors.
   a. Foreign Corrupt Practices Act
   b. Patent
   c. Due diligence
   d. Corporate governance

32. In finance and economics, _____ or divestiture is the reduction of some kind of asset for either financial goals or ethical objectives. A _____ is the opposite of an investment.

Often the term is used as a means to grow financially in which a company sells off a business unit in order to focus their resources on a market it judges to be more profitable, or promising.

a. Portfolio investment
b. Certificate in Investment Performance Measurement
c. Late trading
d. Divestment

33. _____ is an accounting term used to reflect the portion of the book value of a business entity not directly attributable to its assets and liabilities; it normally arises only in case of an acquisition. It reflects the ability of the entity to make a higher profit than would be derived from selling the tangible assets. _____ is also known as an intangible asset.
   a. Consolidation
   b. Net profit
   c. Cost of goods sold
   d. Goodwill

34. A _____ occurs when a financial sponsor acquires a controlling interest in a company's equity and where a significant percentage of the purchase price is financed through leverage (borrowing.) The assets of the acquired company are used as collateral for the borrowed capital, sometimes with assets of the acquiring company. The bonds or other paper issued for _____s are commonly considered not to be investment grade because of the significant risks involved.
   a. Leveraged buyout
   b. Leverage
   c. Limited partnership
   d. Pension fund

35. In law, _____ refers to the process by which a company (or part of a company) is brought to an end, and the assets and property of the company redistributed. _____ can also be referred to as winding-up or dissolution, although dissolution technically refers to the last stage of _____. The process of _____ also arises when customs, an authority or agency in a country responsible for collecting and safeguarding customs duties, determines the final computation or ascertainment of the duties or drawback accruing on an entry.
   a. 4-4-5 Calendar
   b. 529 plan
   c. Debt settlement
   d. Liquidation

36. The phrase _____ refers to the aspect of corporate strategy, corporate finance and management dealing with the buying, selling and combining of different companies that can aid, finance, or help a growing company in a given industry grow rapidly without having to create another business entity.

An acquisition, also known as a takeover, is the buying of one company (the 'target') by another. An acquisition may be friendly or hostile.

   a. 7-Eleven
   b. 529 plan
   c. 4-4-5 Calendar
   d. Mergers and acquisitions

37. A _____ is a new organization or entity formed by a split from a larger one, such as a television series based on a pre-existing one, or a new company formed from a university research group or business incubator. In literature, especially in milieu-based popular fictional book series like mysteries, westerns, fantasy, or science fiction, the term sub-series is generally used instead of _____, but with essentially the same meaning.

_____s as a descriptive term can also include a dissenting faction of a membership organization, a sect of a cult, or a denomination of a church.

   a. 529 plan
   b. 7-Eleven
   c. 4-4-5 Calendar
   d. Spin-off

Chapter 1. An Introduction to Financial Management 9

38. In finance, _____ is the process of estimating the potential market value of a financial asset or liability. they can be done on assets (for example, investments in marketable securities such as stocks, options, business enterprises, or intangible assets such as patents and trademarks) or on liabilities (e.g., Bonds issued by a company.) _____s are required in many contexts including investment analysis, capital budgeting, merger and acquisition transactions, financial reporting, taxable events to determine the proper tax liability, and in litigation.
   a. Valuation
   b. Share
   c. Procter ' Gamble
   d. Margin

39. _____ or financing is to provide capital (funds), which means money for a project, a person, a business or any other private or public institutions.

Those funds can be allocated for either short term or long term purposes. The health fund is a new way of _____ private healthcare centers.

   a. Synthetic CDO
   b. Proxy fight
   c. Funding
   d. Product life cycle

40. _____s are deposits denominated in United States dollars at banks outside the United States, and thus are not under the jurisdiction of the Federal Reserve. Consequently, such deposits are subject to much less regulation than similar deposits within the United States, allowing for higher margins. There is nothing 'European' about _____ deposits; a US dollar-denominated deposit in Tokyo or Caracas would likewise be deemed _____ deposits.
   a. A Random Walk Down Wall Street
   b. Eurodollar
   c. ABN Amro
   d. AAB

41. A _____ is a lease in which the lessor puts up some of the money required to purchase the asset and borrows the rest from a lender. The lender is given a senior secured interest on the asset and an assignment of the lease and lease payments. The lessee makes payments to the lessor, who makes payments to the lender.
   a. Guaranteed consumer funding
   b. Leveraged lease
   c. Debt buyer
   d. Collection agency

42. _____ or net present worth (NPW) is defined as the total present value (PV) of a time series of cash flows. It is a standard method for using the time value of money to appraise long-term projects. Used for capital budgeting, and widely throughout economics, it measures the excess or shortfall of cash flows, in present value terms, once financing charges are met.
   a. Present value of costs
   b. Tax shield
   c. Negative gearing
   d. Net present value

43. An _____ is a lease whose term is short compared to the useful life of the asset or piece of equipment (an airliner, a ship etc.) being leased. An _____ is commonly used to acquire equipment on a relatively short-term basis.
   a. Operating lease
   b. AAB
   c. ABN Amro
   d. A Random Walk Down Wall Street

44. _____ short for sale-and-_____ is a financial transaction, where one sells an asset and leases it back for a long-term: thus one continues to be able to use the asset, but no longer owns it.

Chapter 1. An Introduction to Financial Management

This is generally done for fixed assets, notably real estate and planes, and the purposes are varied, but include financing, accounting, and tax reasons.

After purchasing an asset, the owner enters a long-term agreement by which the property is leased back to the seller, at an agreed-to rate.

a. Leaseback,
c. 4-4-5 Calendar
b. 7-Eleven
d. 529 plan

45. _____ is the process of decreasing an amount over a period of time. The word comes from Middle English amortisen to kill, alienate in mortmain, from Anglo-French amorteser, alteration of amortir, from Vulgar Latin admortire to kill, from Latin ad- + mort-, mors death. Particular instances of the term include:

- _____ (business), the allocation of a lump sum amount to different time periods, particularly for loans and other forms of finance, including related interest or other finance charges.
  - _____ schedule, a table detailing each periodic payment on a loan (typically a mortgage), as generated by an _____ calculator.
  - Negative _____, an _____ schedule where the loan amount actually increases through not paying the full interest
- Amortized analysis, analyzing the execution cost of algorithms over a sequence of operations.
- _____ of capital expenditures of certain assets under accounting rules, particularly intangible assets, in a manner analogous to depreciation.
- _____ (tax law)

_____ is also used in the context of zoning regulations and describes the time in which a property owner has to relocate when the property's use constitutes a preexisting nonconforming use under zoning regulations.

- Depreciation

a. Option
c. AT'T Inc.
b. Intrinsic value
d. Amortization

46. An _____ is a table detailing each periodic payment on a amortizing loan (typically a mortgage), as generated by an amortization calculator.

While a portion of every payment is applied towards both the interest and the principal balance of the loan, the exact amount applied to principal each time varies (with the remainder going to interest.) An _____ reveals the specific monetary amount put towards interest, as well as the specific put towards the Principal balance, with each payment.

a. Annual report
c. Adjusted basis
b. Amortization schedule
d. Adjusting entries

Chapter 1. An Introduction to Financial Management

47. In lending agreements, _____ is a borrower's pledge of specific property to a lender, to secure repayment of a loan. The _____ serves as protection for a lender against a borrower's risk of default - that is, a borrower failing to pay the principal and interest under the terms of a loan obligation. If a borrower does default on a loan (due to insolvency or other event), that borrower forfeits (gives up) the property pledged as _____ *ollateral* - and the lender then becomes the owner of the _____.

   a. Refinancing risk
   b. Nominal value
   c. Collateral
   d. Future-oriented

48. A _____, in its most general sense, is a solemn promise to engage in or refrain from a specified action.

   More specifically, a _____, in contrast to a contract, is a one-way agreement whereby the _____er is the only party bound by the promise. A _____ may have conditions and prerequisites that qualify the undertaking, including the actions of second or third parties, but there is no inherent agreement by such other parties to fulfill those requirements.

   a. Clayton Antitrust Act
   b. Federal Trade Commission Act
   c. Partnership
   d. Covenant

49. Leasing is a process by which a firm can obtain the use of a certain fixed assets for which it must pay a series of contractual, periodic, tax deductable payments. The lessee is the receiver of the services or the assets under the lease contract and the lessor is the owner of the assets. The relationship between the tenant and the landlord is called a _____, and can be for a fixed or an indefinite period of time (called the term of the lease.)

   a. REIT
   b. Real estate investing
   c. Real Estate Investment Trust
   d. Tenancy

50. _____ is a process by which a firm can obtain the use of a certain fixed assets for which it must pay a series of contractual, periodic, tax deductable payments. The lessee is the receiver of the services or the assets under the lease contract and the lessor is the owner of the assets. The relationship between the tenant and the landlord is called a tenancy, and can be for a fixed or an indefinite period of time (called the term of the lease).

   a. Leasing
   b. Foreign Corrupt Practices Act
   c. Quiet period
   d. Royalties

51. In finance, 'participation' is an ownership interest in a mortgage or other loan. In particular, _____ is a cooperation of multiple lenders to issue a loan (known as participation loan) to one borrower. This is usually done in order to reduce individual risks of the lenders.

   a. Short positions
   b. Doctrine of the Proper Law
   c. Securitization
   d. Loan participation

52. _____ is the value on a given date of a future payment or series of future payments, discounted to reflect the time value of money and other factors such as investment risk. _____ calculations are widely used in business and economics to provide a means to compare cash flows at different times on a meaningful 'like to like' basis.

The most commonly applied model of the time value of money is compound interest.

a. Present value
b. Net present value
c. Negative gearing
d. Present value of benefits

Chapter 2. Understanding Financial Statements, Taxes, and Cash Flows

1. In financial accounting, a _____ or statement of financial position is a summary of a person's or organization's balances. Assets, liabilities and ownership equity are listed as of a specific date, such as the end of its financial year. A _____ is often described as a snapshot of a company's financial condition.

   a. Balance sheet
   b. Statement on Auditing Standards No. 70: Service Organizations
   c. Financial statements
   d. Statement of retained earnings

2. _____, refers to consumption opportunity gained by an entity within a specified time frame, which is generally expressed in monetary terms. However, for households and individuals, '_____ is the sum of all the wages, salaries, profits, interests payments, rents and other forms of earnings received... in a given period of time.' For firms, _____ generally refers to net-profit: what remains of revenue after expenses have been subtracted.

   a. Accrual
   b. Annual report
   c. Income
   d. OIBDA

3. An _____ is a financial statement for companies that indicates how Revenue is transformed into net income The purpose of the _____ is to show managers and investors whether the company made or lost money during the period being reported.

   The important thing to remember about an _____ is that it represents a period of time.

   a. Income statement
   b. ABN Amro
   c. AAB
   d. A Random Walk Down Wall Street

4. _____ is the difference between price and the costs of bringing to market whatever it is that is accounted as an enterprise (whether by harvest, extraction, manufacture, or purchase) in terms of the component costs of delivered goods and/or services and any operating or other expenses.

   A key difficulty in measuring profit is in defining costs. Pure economic monetary profits can be zero or negative even in competitive equilibrium when accounted monetized costs exceed monetized price.

   a. Economic profit
   b. AAB
   c. A Random Walk Down Wall Street
   d. Accounting profit

5. _____ is the balance of the amounts of cash being received and paid by a business during a defined period of time, sometimes tied to a specific project. Measurement of _____ can be used

   - to evaluate the state or performance of a business or project.
   - to determine problems with liquidity. Being profitable does not necessarily mean being liquid. A company can fail because of a shortage of cash, even while profitable.
   - to generate project rate of returns. The time of _____s into and out of projects are used as inputs to financial models such as internal rate of return, and net present value.
   - to examine income or growth of a business when it is believed that accrual accounting concepts do not represent economic realities. Alternately, _____ can be used to 'validate' the net income generated by accrual accounting.

   _____ as a generic term may be used differently depending on context, and certain _____ definitions may be adapted by analysts and users for their own uses. Common terms include operating _____ and free _____.

14   *Chapter 2. Understanding Financial Statements, Taxes, and Cash Flows*

_____s can be classified into:

1. Operational _____s: Cash received or expended as a result of the company's core business activities.
2. Investment _____s: Cash received or expended through capital expenditure, investments or acquisitions.
3. Financing _____s: Cash received or expended as a result of financial activities, such as interests and dividends.

All three together - the net _____ - are necessary to reconcile the beginning cash balance to the ending cash balance. Loan draw downs or equity injections, that is just shifting of capital but no expenditure as such, are not considered in the net _____.

   a. Shareholder value   b. Real option
   c. Corporate finance   d. Cash flow

6. In financial and business accounting, _____ is a measure of a firm's profitability that excludes interest and income tax expenses.

EBIT = Operating Revenue - Operating Expenses (OPEX) + Non-operating Income

Operating Income = Operating Revenue - Operating Expenses

Operating income is the difference between operating revenues and operating expenses, but it is also sometimes used as a synonym for EBIT and operating profit. This is true if the firm has no non-operating income.

   a. ABN Amro   b. A Random Walk Down Wall Street
   c. AAB   d. Earnings before interest and taxes

7. _____ is the money retained by the firm before deducting the money to be paid for taxes. _____ includes the money paid for interest. Thus, it can be calculated by subtracting the interest from E.B.I.T (Earnings Before Interest and Taxes)

E.B.T = E.B.I.T - Interest

   a. ABN Amro   b. Earnings before taxes
   c. A Random Walk Down Wall Street   d. AAB

8. _____ is equal to the income that a firm has after subtracting costs and expenses from the total revenue. _____ can be distributed among holders of common stock as a dividend or held by the firm as retained earnings. _____ is an accounting term; in some countries (such as the UK) profit is the usual term.

   a. Historical cost   b. Furniture, Fixtures and Equipment
   c. Net income   d. Write-off

9. _____ is the difference between operating revenues and operating expenses, but it is also sometimes used as a synonym for EBIT and operating profit. This is true if the firm has no non-_____.

A professional investor contemplating a change to the capital structure of a firm (e.g., through a leveraged buyout) first evaluates a firm's fundamental earnings potential (reflected by Earnings Before Interest, Taxes, Depreciation and Amortization EBITDA and EBIT), and then determines the optimal use of debt vs. equity.

   a. AAB
   c. ABN Amro
   b. A Random Walk Down Wall Street
   d. Operating income

10. _____ is a fee paid on borrowed assets. It is the price paid for the use of borrowed money, or, money earned by deposited funds. Assets that are sometimes lent with _____ include money, shares, consumer goods through hire purchase, major assets such as aircraft, and even entire factories in finance lease arrangements.

   a. Insolvency
   c. AAB
   b. Interest
   d. A Random Walk Down Wall Street

11. In business and accounting, _____s are everything of value that is owned by a person or company. The balance sheet of a firm records the monetary value of the _____s owned by the firm. The two major _____ classes are tangible _____s and intangible _____s.

   a. Income
   c. Asset
   b. EBITDA
   d. Accounts payable

12. In accounting, a _____ is an asset on the balance sheet which is expected to be sold or otherwise used up in the near future, usually within one year, or one business cycle - whichever is longer. Typical _____s include cash, cash equivalents, accounts receivable, inventory, the portion of prepaid accounts which will be used within a year, and short-term investments.

On the balance sheet, assets will typically be classified into _____s and long-term assets.

   a. Write-off
   c. Current asset
   b. Long-term liabilities
   d. Historical cost

13. _____ are formal records of a business' financial activities.

16 *Chapter 2. Understanding Financial Statements, Taxes, and Cash Flows*

_____ provide an overview of a business' financial condition in both short and long term. There are four basic _____:

1. **Balance sheet**: also referred to as statement of financial position or condition, reports on a company's assets, liabilities, and net equity as of a given point in time.
2. **Income statement**: also referred to as Profit and Loss statement (or a 'P'L'), reports on a company's income, expenses, and profits over a period of time.
3. **Statement of retained earnings**: explains the changes in a company's retained earnings over the reporting period.
4. **Statement of cash flows**: reports on a company's cash flow activities, particularly its operating, investing and financing activities.

a. Statement of retained earnings

b. Statement on Auditing Standards No. 70: Service Organizations

c. Notes to the Financial Statements

d. Financial statements

14. _____ is a financial metric which represents operating liquidity available to a business. Along with fixed assets such as plant and equipment, _____ is considered a part of operating capital. It is calculated as current assets minus current liabilities.
  a. 4-4-5 Calendar
  b. Working capital management
  c. 529 plan
  d. Working capital

15. _____, in bookkeeping, refers to assets, liabilities, income, and expenses recorded on individual pages of the so called book of final entry or ledger. Changes in _____ value are made by chronologically posting debit (DR) and credit (CR) entries to its page. Examples of _____s are cash, _____s receivable, mortgages, loans, land and buildings, common stock, sales, services provided, wages, and payroll overhead.
  a. Account
  b. Option
  c. Accretion
  d. Alpha

16. _____ is one of a series of accounting transactions dealing with the billing of customers who owe money to a person, company or organization for goods and services that have been provided to the customer. In most business entities this is typically done by generating an invoice and mailing or electronically delivering it to the customer, who in turn must pay it within an established timeframe called credit or payment terms.

An example of a common payment term is Net 30, meaning payment is due in the amount of the invoice 30 days from the date of invoice.

  a. Accounting methods
  b. Income
  c. Impaired asset
  d. Accounts receivable

17. _____ is a list for goods and materials held available in stock by a business. It is also used for a list of the contents of a household and for a list for testamentary purposes of the possessions of someone who has died. In accounting _____ is considered an asset.

Chapter 2. Understanding Financial Statements, Taxes, and Cash Flows 17

    a. ABN Amro
    b. A Random Walk Down Wall Street
    c. Inventory
    d. AAB

18. _____ plant, and equipment, is a term used in accountancy for assets and property which cannot easily be converted into cash. This can be compared with current assets such as cash or bank accounts, which are described as liquid assets. In most cases, only tangible assets are referred to as fixed.
    a. Percentage of Completion
    b. Petty cash
    c. Remittance advice
    d. Fixed asset

19. _____ are defined as identifiable non-monetary assets that cannot be seen, touched or physically measured, which are created through time and/or effort and that are identifiable as a separate asset. There are two primary forms of intangibles - legal intangibles (such as trade secrets (e.g., customer lists), copyrights, patents, trademarks, and goodwill) and competitive intangibles (such as knowledge activities (know-how, knowledge), collaboration activities, leverage activities, and structural activities.) Legal intangibles generate legal property rights defensible in a court of law.
    a. ABN Amro
    b. Intangible assets
    c. A Random Walk Down Wall Street
    d. AAB

20. In accounting, _____ or *Carrying value* is the value of an asset according to its balance sheet account balance. For assets, the value is based on the original cost of the asset less any depreciation, amortization or impairment costs made against the asset. A company's _____ is its total assets minus intangible assets and liabilities.
    a. Retained earnings
    b. Pro forma
    c. Current liabilities
    d. Book value

21. _____ is a file or account that contains money that a person or company owes to suppliers, but hasn't paid yet (a form of debt.) When you receive an invoice you add it to the file, and then you remove it when you pay. Thus, the A/P is a form of credit that suppliers offer to their purchasers by allowing them to pay for a product or service after it has already been received.
    a. Outstanding balance
    b. Earnings before interest, taxes, depreciation and amortization
    c. Accrual
    d. Accounts payable

22. In United States banking, _____ is a marketing term for certain services offered primarily to larger business customers. It may be used to describe all bank accounts (such as checking accounts) provided to businesses of a certain size, but it is more often used to describe specific services such as cash concentration, zero balance accounting, and automated clearing house facilities. Sometimes, private banking customers are given _____ services.
    a. Cash management
    b. Capitalization rate
    c. Profitability index
    d. Global tactical asset allocation

23. _____ is that which is owed; usually referencing assets owed, but the term can cover other obligations. In the case of assets, _____ is a means of using future purchasing power in the present before a summation has been earned. Some companies and corporations use _____ as a part of their overall corporate finance strategy.
    a. Debt
    b. Credit cycle
    c. Partial Payment
    d. Cross-collateralization

Chapter 2. Understanding Financial Statements, Taxes, and Cash Flows

24. _____ is the capital that a business raises by taking out a loan. It is a loan made to a company that is normally repaid at some future date. _____ differs from equity or share capital because subscribers to _____ do not become part owners of the business, but are merely creditors, and the suppliers of _____ usually receive a contractually fixed annual percentage return on their loan, and this is known as the coupon rate.
   a. Debt capital
   b. Financial assistance
   c. Risk-return spectrum
   d. Floating charge

25. In economic models, the _____ time frame assumes no fixed factors of production. Firms can enter or leave the marketplace, and the cost (and availability) of land, labor, raw materials, and capital goods can be assumed to vary. In contrast, in the short-run time frame, certain factors are assumed to be fixed, because there is not sufficient time for them to change.
   a. Short-run
   b. 4-4-5 Calendar
   c. 529 plan
   d. Long-run

26. _____, in finance and accounting, means stated value or face value. From this comes the expressions at par (at the _____), over par (over _____) and under par (under _____.)

The term '_____' has several meanings depending on context and geography.

   a. Sinking fund
   b. Par value
   c. FIDC
   d. Global Squeeze

27. In accounting, _____ refers to the portion of net income which is retained by the corporation rather than distributed to its owners as dividends. Similarly, if the corporation makes a loss, then that loss is retained and called variously retained losses, accumulated losses or accumulated deficit. _____ and losses are cumulative from year to year with losses offsetting earnings.
   a. Generally Accepted Accounting Principles
   b. Retained earnings
   c. Historical cost
   d. Matching principle

28. In economics, the concept of the _____ refers to the decision-making time frame of a firm in which at least one factor of production is fixed. Costs which are fixed in the _____ have no impact on a firms decisions. For example a firm can raise output by increasing the amount of labour through overtime.
   a. 529 plan
   b. Short-run
   c. Long-run
   d. 4-4-5 Calendar

29. A _____ or reacquired stock is stock which is bought back by the issuing company, reducing the amount of outstanding stock on the open market ('open market' including insiders' holdings.)

Stock repurchases are often used as a tax-efficient method to put cash into shareholders' hands, rather than pay dividends. Sometimes, companies do this when they feel that their stock is undervalued on the open market.

   a. Trial balance
   b. Treasury stock
   c. Current asset
   d. Generally Accepted Accounting Principles

Chapter 2. Understanding Financial Statements, Taxes, and Cash Flows

30. A mutual shareholder or _____ is an individual or company (including a corporation) that legally owns one or more shares of stock in a joint stock company. A company's shareholders collectively own that company. Thus, the typical goal of such companies is to enhance shareholder value.
    a. Stock market bubble
    b. Limit order
    c. Trading curb
    d. Stockholder

31. _____ is a measure of the ability of a debtor to pay their debts as and when they fall due. It is usually expressed as a ratio or a percentage of current liabilities.

    For a corporation with a published balance sheet there are various ratios used to calculate a measure of liquidity.

    a. Invested capital
    b. Operating leverage
    c. Accounting liquidity
    d. Operating profit margin

32. _____ refers to a tax levied by various jurisdictions on the profits made by companies or associations. It is a tax on the value of the corporation's profits.

    The measure of taxable profits varies from country to country.

    a. Proxy fight
    b. First-mover advantage
    c. Trade finance
    d. Corporate tax

33. _____ is a term used in accounting, economics and finance to spread the cost of an asset over the span of several years.

    In simple words we can say that _____ is the reduction in the value of an asset due to usage, passage of time, wear and tear, technological outdating or obsolescence, depletion or other such factors.

    In accounting, _____ is a term used to describe any method of attributing the historical or purchase cost of an asset across its useful life, roughly corresponding to normal wear and tear.

    a. Deferred financing costs
    b. Bottom line
    c. Matching principle
    d. Depreciation

34. _____ is commonly defined as the amount of a company's or a person's income before all deductions or any taxpayer's income, except that which is specifically excluded by the Internal Revenue Code, before taking deductions or taxes into account. For a business, this amount is pre-tax net sales less cost of sales. Section 61 of the Internal Revenue Code (Code) defines '_____' as 'all income from whatever source derived.' Section 61(a) of the Code lists fifteen examples of items included in _____; however, the list is not exhaustive.
    a. Gross income
    b. Financial distress
    c. Shareholder value
    d. Second lien loan

Chapter 2. Understanding Financial Statements, Taxes, and Cash Flows

35. Depreciation methods that provide for a higher depreciation charge in the first year of an asset's life and gradually decreasing charges in subsequent years are called accelerated depreciation methods. This may be a more realistic reflection of an asset's actual expected benefit from the use of the asset: many assets are most useful when they are new. One popular accelerated method is the declining-balance method. Under this method the Book Value is multiplied by a fixed rate.

The most common rate used is double the straight-line rate. For this reason, this technique is referred to as the _____. To illustrate, suppose a business has an asset with $1,000 Original Cost, $100 Salvage Value, and 5 years useful life. First, calculate straight-line depreciation rate. Since the asset has 5 years useful life, the straight-line depreciation rate equals (100% / 5) 20% per year. With _____, as the name suggests, double that rate, or 40% depreciation rate is used.

- a. Doctrine of the Proper Law
- b. Database auditing
- c. The Goodyear Tire ' Rubber Company
- d. Double-declining-balance method

36. _____ is the portion of income that is the subject of taxation according to the laws that determine what is income and the taxation rate for that income. Generally, _____ refers to an individual's (or corporation's) gross income, adjusted for various deductions allowable by statute. The main questions put by most individuals in any jurisdiction are 'what makes up my _____' and what tax rates should be applied such that I can work out my tax liability to the state.

- a. 529 plan
- b. 4-4-5 Calendar
- c. 7-Eleven
- d. Taxable income

37. In financial accounting, a _____ or statement of cash flows is a financial statement that shows a company's flow of cash. The money coming into the business is called cash inflow, and money going out from the business is called cash outflow. The statement shows how changes in balance sheet and income accounts affect cash and cash equivalents, and breaks the analysis down to operating, investing, and financing activities.

- a. 529 plan
- b. Cash flow statement
- c. 4-4-5 Calendar
- d. 7-Eleven

38. Earnings before interest, taxes, depreciation and amortization (_____) is a non-GAAP metric that can be used to evaluate a company's profitability.

_____ = Operating Revenue - Operating Expenses + Other Revenue

Its name comes from the fact that Operating Expenses do not include interest, taxes, or amortization. _____ is not a defined measure according to Generally Accepted Accounting Principles (GAAP), and thus can be calculated however a company wishes.

- a. Accounts payable
- b. Invoice processing
- c. Accrual
- d. EBITDA

39. In corporate finance, _____ is a cash flow available for distribution among all the security holders of a company. They include equity holders, debt holders, preferred stock holders, convertible security holders, and so on.

Note that the first three lines above are calculated for you on the standard Statement of Cash Flows.

Chapter 2. Understanding Financial Statements, Taxes, and Cash Flows

a. Funding
b. Forfaiting
c. Safety stock
d. Free cash flow

40. _____ is the process of decreasing an amount over a period of time. The word comes from Middle English amortisen to kill, alienate in mortmain, from Anglo-French amorteser, alteration of amortir, from Vulgar Latin admortire to kill, from Latin ad- + mort-, mors death. Particular instances of the term include:

- _____ (business), the allocation of a lump sum amount to different time periods, particularly for loans and other forms of finance, including related interest or other finance charges.
    - _____ schedule, a table detailing each periodic payment on a loan (typically a mortgage), as generated by an _____ calculator.
    - Negative _____, an _____ schedule where the loan amount actually increases through not paying the full interest
- Amortized analysis, analyzing the execution cost of algorithms over a sequence of operations.
- _____ of capital expenditures of certain assets under accounting rules, particularly intangible assets, in a manner analogous to depreciation.
- _____ (tax law)

_____ is also used in the context of zoning regulations and describes the time in which a property owner has to relocate when the property's use constitutes a preexisting nonconforming use under zoning regulations.

- Depreciation

a. AT'T Inc.
b. Amortization
c. Intrinsic value
d. Option

41. _____ is the planning process used to determine whether a firm's long term investments such as new machinery, replacement machinery, new plants, new products, and research development projects are worth pursuing. It is budget for major capital, or investment, expenditures.

Many formal methods are used in _____, including the techniques such as

- Net present value
- Profitability index
- Internal rate of return
- Modified Internal Rate of Return
- Equivalent annuity

These methods use the incremental cash flows from each potential investment, or project. Techniques based on accounting earnings and accounting rules are sometimes used - though economists consider this to be improper - such as the accounting rate of return, and 'return on investment.' Simplified and hybrid methods are used as well, such as payback period and discounted payback period.

Chapter 2. Understanding Financial Statements, Taxes, and Cash Flows

a. Financial distress
b. Shareholder value
c. Capital budgeting
d. Preferred stock

42. In accounting, _____ are considered liabilities of the business that are to be settled in cash within the fiscal year or the operating cycle, whichever period is longer.

For example accounts payable for goods, services or supplies that were purchased for use in the operation of the business and payable within a normal period of time would be _____.

Bonds, mortgages and loans that are payable over a term exceeding one year would be fixed liabilities.

a. Gross sales
b. Current liabilities
c. Net income
d. Closing entries

43. _____ or financing is to provide capital (funds), which means money for a project, a person, a business or any other private or public institutions.

Those funds can be allocated for either short term or long term purposes. The health fund is a new way of _____ private healthcare centers.

a. Synthetic CDO
b. Product life cycle
c. Proxy fight
d. Funding

44. The role of the _____ is to issue accounting standards in the United Kingdom. It is recognised for that purpose under the Companies Act 1985. It took over the task of setting accounting standards from the Accounting Standards Committee (ASC) in 1990.

a. A Random Walk Down Wall Street
b. AAB
c. ABN Amro
d. Accounting Standards Board

45. _____ is the standard framework of guidelines for financial accounting used in the United States of America. It includes the standards, conventions, and rules accountants follow in recording and summarizing transactions, and in the preparation of financial statements. _____ are now issued by the Financial Accounting Standards Board (FASB).

a. Generally Accepted Accounting Principles
b. Revenue
c. Depreciation
d. Net income

46. The _____ founded on April 1, 2001 is the successor of the International Accounting Standards Committee (IASC) founded in June 1973 in London. It is responsible for developing the International Financial Reporting Standards (new name for the International Accounting Standards issued after 2001), and promoting the use and application of these standards.

The _____ is an independent, privately-funded accounting standard-setter based in London, UK.

a. American Accounting Association
b. Association of Certified Public Accountants
c. International Federation of Accountants
d. International Accounting Standards Board

47. The _____ is a private, not-for-profit organization whose primary purpose is to develop generally accepted accounting principles (GAAP) within the United States in the public's interest. The Securities and Exchange Commission (SEC) designated the _____ as the organization responsible for setting accounting standards for public companies in the U.S. It was created in 1973, replacing the Accounting Principles Board and the Committee on Accounting Procedure of the American Institute of Certified Public Accountants. The _____'s mission is 'to establish and improve standards of financial accounting and reporting for the guidance and education of the public, including issuers, auditors, and users of financial information.'

The _____ is not a governmental body.

   a. MRU Holdings   b. FASB
   c. PlaNet Finance   d. Credit karma

48. _____ is the field of accountancy concerned with the preparation of financial statements for decision makers, such as stockholders, suppliers, banks, employees, government agencies, owners, and other stakeholders. The fundamental need for _____ is to reduce principal-agent problem by measuring and monitoring agents' performance and reporting the results to interested users.

_____ is used to prepare accounting information for people outside the organization or not involved in the day to day running of the company.

   a. 7-Eleven   b. 4-4-5 Calendar
   c. 529 plan   d. Financial Accounting

49. The _____ is a private, not-for-profit organization whose primary purpose is to develop generally accepted accounting principles (GAAP) within the United States in the public's interest. The Securities and Exchange Commission (SEC) designated the _____ as the organization responsible for setting accounting standards for public companies in the U.S. It was created in 1973, replacing the Accounting Principles Board and the Committee on Accounting Procedure of the American Institute of Certified Public Accountants. The _____'s mission is 'to establish and improve standards of financial accounting and reporting for the guidance and education of the public, including issuers, auditors, and users of financial information.'

The _____ is not a governmental body.

   a. Federal Deposit Insurance Corporation   b. World Congress of Accountants
   c. KPMG   d. Financial Accounting Standards Board

Chapter 3. Evaluating a Firm's Financial Performance

1. In finance, a _____ or accounting ratio is a ratio of two selected numerical values taken from an enterprise's financial statements. There are many standard ratios used to try to evaluate the overall financial condition of a corporation or other organization. They may be used by managers within a firm, by current and potential shareholders (owners) of a firm, and by a firm's creditors. Security analysts use these to compare the strengths and weaknesses in various companies.
   a. Sustainable growth rate
   b. Financial ratio
   c. Price/cash flow ratio
   d. Return on capital employed

2. In finance, the Acid-test or _____ or liquid ratio measures the ability of a company to use its near cash or quick assets to immediately extinguish or retire its current liabilities. Quick assets include those current assets that presumably can be quickly converted to cash at close to their book values.

Generally, the acid test ratio should be 1:1 or better, however this varies widely by industry.

   a. P/E ratio
   b. Quick ratio
   c. Financial ratio
   d. Net assets

3. The _____ is a financial ratio that measures whether or not a firm has enough resources to pay its debts over the next 12 months. It compares a firm's current assets to its current liabilities. It is expressed as follows:

$$\text{Current ratio} = \frac{\text{Current Assets}}{\text{Current Liabilities}}$$

For example, if WXY Company's current assets are $50,000,000 and its current liabilities are $40,000,000, then its _____ would be $50,000,000 divided by $40,000,000, which equals 1.25.

   a. Current ratio
   b. Debt service coverage ratio
   c. PEG ratio
   d. Sustainable growth rate

4. _____ is a measure of the ability of a debtor to pay their debts as and when they fall due. It is usually expressed as a ratio or a percentage of current liabilities.

For a corporation with a published balance sheet there are various ratios used to calculate a measure of liquidity.

   a. Operating profit margin
   b. Invested capital
   c. Operating leverage
   d. Accounting liquidity

5. _____, in bookkeeping, refers to assets, liabilities, income, and expenses recorded on individual pages of the so called book of final entry or ledger. Changes in _____ value are made by chronologically posting debit (DR) and credit (CR) entries to its page. Examples of _____s are cash, _____s receivable, mortgages, loans, land and buildings, common stock, sales, services provided, wages, and payroll overhead.
   a. Alpha
   b. Account
   c. Accretion
   d. Option

Chapter 3. Evaluating a Firm's Financial Performance

6. _____ is one of a series of accounting transactions dealing with the billing of customers who owe money to a person, company or organization for goods and services that have been provided to the customer. In most business entities this is typically done by generating an invoice and mailing or electronically delivering it to the customer, who in turn must pay it within an established timeframe called credit or payment terms.

An example of a common payment term is Net 30, meaning payment is due in the amount of the invoice 30 days from the date of invoice.

   a. Income   b. Accounting methods
   c. Accounts receivable   d. Impaired asset

7. _____ is one of the accounting liquidity ratios, a financial ratio. This ratio measures the number of times, on average, receivables (e.g. Accounts Receivable) are collected during the period. A popular variant of the _____ is to convert it into an Average Collection Period in terms of days.

   a. Return on equity   b. Sharpe ratio
   c. PEG ratio   d. Receivables turnover ratio

8. _____ is a list for goods and materials held available in stock by a business. It is also used for a list of the contents of a household and for a list for testamentary purposes of the possessions of someone who has died. In accounting _____ is considered an asset.

   a. ABN Amro   b. A Random Walk Down Wall Street
   c. AAB   d. Inventory

9. The _____ is an equation that equals the cost of goods sold divided by the average inventory. Average inventory equals beginning inventory plus ending inventory divided by 2.

The formula for _____ :

$$\text{Inventory Turnover} = \frac{\text{Cost of Goods Sold}}{\text{Average Inventory}}$$

The formula for average inventory:

$$\text{Average Inventory} = \frac{\text{Beginning inventory} + \text{Ending inventory}}{2}$$

A low turnover rate may point to overstocking, obsolescence, or deficiencies in the product line or marketing effort.

   a. Operating leverage   b. Inventory turnover
   c. Earnings yield   d. Information ratio

10. _____ is one of the Accounting Liquidity ratios, a financial ratio. This ratio measures the number of times, on average, the inventory is sold during the period. Its purpose is to measure the liquidity of the inventory.

Chapter 3. Evaluating a Firm's Financial Performance

a. AAB
c. A Random Walk Down Wall Street
b. ABN Amro
d. Inventory turnover ratio

11. _____ is the difference between operating revenues and operating expenses, but it is also sometimes used as a synonym for EBIT and operating profit. This is true if the firm has no non-_____.

A professional investor contemplating a change to the capital structure of a firm (e.g., through a leveraged buyout) first evaluates a firm's fundamental earnings potential (reflected by Earnings Before Interest, Taxes, Depreciation and Amortization EBITDA and EBIT), and then determines the optimal use of debt vs. equity.

a. ABN Amro
c. A Random Walk Down Wall Street
b. Operating income
d. AAB

12. _____, refers to consumption opportunity gained by an entity within a specified time frame, which is generally expressed in monetary terms. However, for households and individuals, '_____ is the sum of all the wages, salaries, profits, interests payments, rents and other forms of earnings received... in a given period of time.' For firms, _____ generally refers to net-profit: what remains of revenue after expenses have been subtracted.

a. Annual report
c. OIBDA
b. Accrual
d. Income

13. In finance, _____, also known as return on investment is the ratio of money gained or lost on an investment relative to the amount of money invested. The amount of money gained or lost may be referred to as interest, profit/loss, gain/loss, or net income/loss. The money invested may be referred to as the asset, capital, principal, or the cost basis of the investment.

a. Stock or scrip dividends
c. Composiition of Creditors
b. Doctrine of the Proper Law
d. Rate of return

14. _____ is a measure of a company's earning power from ongoing operations, equal to earnings before the deduction of interest payments and income taxes.

To accountants, economic profit, or EP, is a single-period metric to determine the value created by a company in one period - usually a year. It is the net profit after tax less the equity charge, a risk-weighted cost of capital.

a. A Random Walk Down Wall Street
c. AAB
b. Operating profit
d. Economic profit

15. In business, operating margin, operating income margin, _____ or return on sales (ROS) is the ratio of operating income (operating profit in the UK) divided by net sales, usually presented in percent.

(Relevant figures in italics)

Chapter 3. Evaluating a Firm`s Financial Performance

It is a measurement of what proportion of a company's revenue is left over, before taxes and other indirect costs (such as rent, bonus, interest, etc.), after paying for variable costs of production as wages, raw materials, etc. A good operating margin is needed for a company to be able to pay for its fixed costs, such as interest on debt.

a. Average rate of return
b. Interest coverage ratio
c. Operating leverage
d. Operating profit margin

16. In finance, a _____ is collateral that the holder of a position in securities, options, or futures contracts has to deposit to cover the credit risk of his counterparty (most often his broker.) This risk can arise if the holder has done any of the following:

- borrowed cash from the counterparty to buy securities or options,
- sold securities or options short, or
- entered into a futures contract.

The collateral can be in the form of cash or securities, and it is deposited in a _____ account. On U.S. futures exchanges, '_____' was formally called performance bond.

_____ buying is buying securities with cash borrowed from a broker, using other securities as collateral.

a. Share
b. Procter ' Gamble
c. Credit
d. Margin

17. _____ is the difference between price and the costs of bringing to market whatever it is that is accounted as an enterprise (whether by harvest, extraction, manufacture, or purchase) in terms of the component costs of delivered goods and/or services and any operating or other expenses.

A key difficulty in measuring profit is in defining costs. Pure economic monetary profits can be zero or negative even in competitive equilibrium when accounted monetized costs exceed monetized price.

a. Economic profit
b. A Random Walk Down Wall Street
c. Accounting profit
d. AAB

18. _____, Net Margin, Net _____ or Net Profit Ratio all refer to a measure of profitability. It is calculated using a formula and written as a percentage or a number.

$$\text{Net profit margin} = \frac{\text{Net profit after taxes}}{\text{Net Sales}}$$

The _____ is mostly used for internal comparison.

a. Profit margin
b. Profit maximization
c. 4-4-5 Calendar
d. Net profit margin

Chapter 3. Evaluating a Firm's Financial Performance

19. _____ plant, and equipment, is a term used in accountancy for assets and property which cannot easily be converted into cash. This can be compared with current assets such as cash or bank accounts, which are described as liquid assets. In most cases, only tangible assets are referred to as fixed.
   - a. Percentage of Completion
   - b. Remittance advice
   - c. Petty cash
   - d. Fixed asset

20. In business and accounting, _____s are everything of value that is owned by a person or company. The balance sheet of a firm records the monetary value of the _____s owned by the firm. The two major _____ classes are tangible _____s and intangible _____s.
   - a. Income
   - b. EBITDA
   - c. Accounts payable
   - d. Asset

21. _____ is a financial ratio that measures the efficiency of a company's use of its assets in generating sales revenue or sales income to the company.

$$Asset\ Turnover = \frac{Sales}{Average\ Total\ Assets}$$

- 'Sales' is the value of 'Net Sales' or 'Sales' from the company's income statement
- 'Average Total Assets' is the value of 'Total assets' from the company's balance sheet in the beginning and the end of the fiscal period divided by 2.

- Assets turnover

   - a. Asset turnover
   - b. Inventory turnover
   - c. Earnings yield
   - d. Average accounting return

22. _____ is a business term and may be used as a broad measure of asset efficiency and is calculated by dividing sales revenue by the total assets.

It's also used in the Du Pont Identity:

$$\frac{Net\ Earnings}{Shareholders\ Eq.} = \frac{Net\ Earnings}{Sales(Income)} * \frac{Sales(Income)}{Total\ Assets} * \frac{Total\ Assets}{Shareholders\ Eq.}$$

In which,

$$Net\ Margin = \frac{Net\ Earnings}{Sales(Income)}$$

$$Total\ Asset\ Turnover = \frac{Sales(Income)}{Total\ Assets}$$

$$Financial\ Leverage = \frac{Average\ Total\ Assets}{Average\ Total\ Equity}$$

The net margin is a summary indicator of an income statement, Asset turnover is an indicator of the left side of the balance sheet (total assets' side) and Leverage is an indicator of the right side of the Balance Sheet (liabilities and shareholders' equity' side.)

The Du Pont Identity helps many companies or individuals, visualize and comprehend the analysis of a financial statement or annual report of a company, in return on assets and return on investments.

a. Operating profit margin
b. Earnings yield
c. Invested capital
d. Assets turnover

23. _____ is that which is owed; usually referencing assets owed, but the term can cover other obligations. In the case of assets, _____ is a means of using future purchasing power in the present before a summation has been earned. Some companies and corporations use _____ as a part of their overall corporate finance strategy.
a. Credit cycle
b. Partial Payment
c. Cross-collateralization
d. Debt

24. _____ is a financial ratio that indicates the percentage of a company's assets are provided via debt. It is the ratio of total debt (the sum of current liabilities and long-term liabilities) and total assets (the sum of current assets, fixed assets, and other assets such as 'goodwill'.)

or alternatively:

For example, a company with $2 million in total assets and $500,000 in total liabilities would have a _____ of 25%

Like all financial ratios, a company's _____ should be compared with their industry average or other competing firms.

a. Cash concentration
b. Capitalization rate
c. Cash management
d. Debt ratio

25. _____ or financing is to provide capital (funds), which means money for a project, a person, a business or any other private or public institutions.

Those funds can be allocated for either short term or long term purposes. The health fund is a new way of _____ private healthcare centers.

a. Proxy fight
b. Synthetic CDO
c. Product life cycle
d. Funding

26. _____ measures the rate of return on the ownership interest (shareholders' equity) of the common stock owners. _____ is viewed as one of the most important financial ratios. It measures a firm's efficiency at generating profits from every dollar of shareholders' equity (also known as net assets or assets minus liabilities.)

a. Return on sales
b. Diluted Earnings Per Share
c. Return of capital
d. Return on equity

27. The _____ percentage shows how profitable a company's assets are in generating revenue.

_____ can be computed as:

$$ROA = \frac{\text{Net Income}}{\text{Total Assets}}$$

This number tells you 'what the company can do with what it's got', i.e. how many dollars of earnings they derive from each dollar of assets they control. It's a useful number for comparing competing companies in the same industry.

a. Return on assets
b. Return on sales
c. Receivables turnover ratio
d. P/E ratio

28. _____ or interest coverage ratio is a measure of a company's ability to honor its debt payments. It may be calculated as either EBIT or EBITDA divided by the total interest payable.

$$\text{Times-Interest-Earned} = \frac{\text{EBIT or EBITDA}}{\text{Interest Charges}}$$

- Financial ratio
- Financial leverage
- EBIT
- EBITDA
- Debt service coverage ratio

Interest Charges = Traditionally 'charges' refers to interest expense found on the income statement.

_____ or Interest Coverage is a great tool when measuring a company's ability to meet its debt obligations.

a. Net assets
b. Cash conversion cycle
c. Times interest earned
d. Return of capital

29. _____ is a fee paid on borrowed assets. It is the price paid for the use of borrowed money, or, money earned by deposited funds. Assets that are sometimes lent with _____ include money, shares, consumer goods through hire purchase, major assets such as aircraft, and even entire factories in finance lease arrangements.

a. AAB
c. Insolvency

b. A Random Walk Down Wall Street
d. Interest

Chapter 4. Financial Forecasting, Planning, and Budgeting

1. In financial accounting, a _____ or statement of financial position is a summary of a person's or organization's balances. Assets, liabilities and ownership equity are listed as of a specific date, such as the end of its financial year. A _____ is often described as a snapshot of a company's financial condition.

   a. Statement of retained earnings
   b. Statement on Auditing Standards No. 70: Service Organizations
   c. Financial statements
   d. Balance sheet

2. The term _____ is a term applied to practices that are perfunctory, or seek to satisfy the minimum requirements or to conform to a convention or doctrine. It has different meanings in different fields.

   In accounting, _____ earnings are those earnings of companies in addition to actual earnings calculated under the Generally Accepted Accounting Principles (GAAP) in their quarterly and yearly financial reports.

   a. Pro forma
   b. Deferred financing costs
   c. Long-term liabilities
   d. Deferred income

3. _____ is the balance of the amounts of cash being received and paid by a business during a defined period of time, sometimes tied to a specific project. Measurement of _____ can be used

   - to evaluate the state or performance of a business or project.
   - to determine problems with liquidity. Being profitable does not necessarily mean being liquid. A company can fail because of a shortage of cash, even while profitable.
   - to generate project rate of returns. The time of _____s into and out of projects are used as inputs to financial models such as internal rate of return, and net present value.
   - to examine income or growth of a business when it is believed that accrual accounting concepts do not represent economic realities. Alternately, _____ can be used to 'validate' the net income generated by accrual accounting.

   _____ as a generic term may be used differently depending on context, and certain _____ definitions may be adapted by analysts and users for their own uses. Common terms include operating _____ and free _____.

   _____s can be classified into:

   1. Operational _____s: Cash received or expended as a result of the company's core business activities.
   2. Investment _____s: Cash received or expended through capital expenditure, investments or acquisitions.
   3. Financing _____s: Cash received or expended as a result of financial activities, such as interests and dividends.

   All three together - the net _____ - are necessary to reconcile the beginning cash balance to the ending cash balance. Loan draw downs or equity injections, that is just shifting of capital but no expenditure as such, are not considered in the net _____.

   a. Real option
   b. Cash flow
   c. Corporate finance
   d. Shareholder value

Chapter 4. Financial Forecasting, Planning, and Budgeting

4. _____ are formal records of a business' financial activities.

_____ provide an overview of a business' financial condition in both short and long term. There are four basic _____:

1. **Balance sheet**: also referred to as statement of financial position or condition, reports on a company's assets, liabilities, and net equity as of a given point in time.
2. **Income statement**: also referred to as Profit and Loss statement (or a 'P'L'), reports on a company's income, expenses, and profits over a period of time.
3. **Statement of retained earnings**: explains the changes in a company's retained earnings over the reporting period.
4. **Statement of cash flows**: reports on a company's cash flow activities, particularly its operating, investing and financing activities.

a. Notes to the Financial Statements
b. Statement on Auditing Standards No. 70: Service Organizations
c. Statement of retained earnings
d. Financial statements

5. _____ or financing is to provide capital (funds), which means money for a project, a person, a business or any other private or public institutions.

Those funds can be allocated for either short term or long term purposes. The health fund is a new way of _____ private healthcare centers.

a. Funding
b. Proxy fight
c. Product life cycle
d. Synthetic CDO

6. In business and finance accounting, _____ is equal to the gross profit minus overheads minus interest payable plus/minus one off items for a given time period (usually: accounting period.)

A common synonym for '_____' when discussing financial statements (which include a balance sheet and an income statement) is the bottom line. This term results from the traditional appearance of an income statement which shows all allocated revenues and expenses over a specified time period with the resulting summation on the bottom line of the report.

a. Deferred
b. Gross sales
c. Net profit
d. Salvage value

7. Profit margin, net margin, _____ or net profit ratio all refer to a measure of profitability. It is calculated by finding the net profit as a percentage of the revenue.

The profit margin is mostly used for internal comparison.

a. Profit margin
c. Profit maximization
b. 4-4-5 Calendar
d. Net profit margin

8. In finance, a _____ is collateral that the holder of a position in securities, options, or futures contracts has to deposit to cover the credit risk of his counterparty (most often his broker.) This risk can arise if the holder has done any of the following:

- borrowed cash from the counterparty to buy securities or options,
- sold securities or options short, or
- entered into a futures contract.

The collateral can be in the form of cash or securities, and it is deposited in a _____ account. On U.S. futures exchanges, '_____' was formally called performance bond.

_____ buying is buying securities with cash borrowed from a broker, using other securities as collateral.

a. Credit
c. Procter ' Gamble
b. Margin
d. Share

9. _____ is the difference between price and the costs of bringing to market whatever it is that is accounted as an enterprise (whether by harvest, extraction, manufacture, or purchase) in terms of the component costs of delivered goods and/or services and any operating or other expenses.

A key difficulty in measuring profit is in defining costs. Pure economic monetary profits can be zero or negative even in competitive equilibrium when accounted monetized costs exceed monetized price.

a. AAB
c. Economic profit
b. A Random Walk Down Wall Street
d. Accounting profit

10. _____, Net Margin, Net _____ or Net Profit Ratio all refer to a measure of profitability. It is calculated using a formula and written as a percentage or a number.

$$\text{Net profit margin} = \frac{\text{Net profit after taxes}}{\text{Net Sales}}$$

The _____ is mostly used for internal comparison.

a. 4-4-5 Calendar
c. Net profit margin
b. Profit maximization
d. Profit margin

11. A _____ is a payment made by a corporation to its shareholder members. When a corporation earns a profit or surplus, that money can be put to two uses: it can either be re-invested in the business (called retained earnings), or it can be paid to the shareholders as a _____. Many corporations retain a portion of their earnings and pay the remainder as a _____.

Chapter 4. Financial Forecasting, Planning, and Budgeting

a. Special dividend
b. Dividend yield
c. Dividend puzzle
d. Dividend

12. _____ is the fraction of net income a firm pays to its stockholders in dividends:

The part of the earnings not paid to investors is left for investment to provide for future earnings growth. Investors seeking high current income and limited capital growth prefer companies with high _____. However investors seeking capital growth may prefer lower payout ratio because capital gains are taxed at a lower rate.

a. Dividend imputation
b. Dividend puzzle
c. Dividend yield
d. Dividend payout ratio

13. _____, in microeconomics, are the cost advantages that a business obtains due to expansion. _____ may be utilized by any size firm expanding its scale of operation.

a. Employee Retirement Income Security Act
b. Uniform Commercial Code
c. Articles of incorporation
d. Economies of scale

14. In business and accounting, _____s are everything of value that is owned by a person or company. The balance sheet of a firm records the monetary value of the _____s owned by the firm. The two major _____ classes are tangible _____s and intangible _____s.

a. Asset
b. EBITDA
c. Accounts payable
d. Income

15. _____ measures the rate of return on the ownership interest (shareholders' equity) of the common stock owners. _____ is viewed as one of the most important financial ratios. It measures a firm's efficiency at generating profits from every dollar of shareholders' equity (also known as net assets or assets minus liabilities.)

a. Return of capital
b. Return on sales
c. Diluted Earnings Per Share
d. Return on equity

16. _____ is the task of determining how a business will afford to achieve its strategic goals and objectives. Usually, a company creates a Financial Plan immediately after the vision and objectives have been set. The Financial Plan describes each of the activities, resources, equipment and materials that are needed to achieve these objectives, as well as the timeframes involved.

a. Corporate Transparency
b. Financial planning
c. Performance measurement
d. Management by exception

17. Working capital requirements of a business should be monitored at all times to ensure that there are sufficient funds available to meet short-term expenses.

The _____ is basically a detailed plan that shows all expected sources and uses of cash

Chapter 4. Financial Forecasting, Planning, and Budgeting

a. Mitigating Control
c. Cash budget
b. Loans and interest, in Judaism
d. Rate of return

18. The _____ of 1977 (15 U.S.C. §§ 78dd-1, et seq.) is a United States federal law known primarily for two of its main provisions, one that addresses accounting transparency requirements under the Securities Exchange Act of 1934 and another concerning bribery of foreign officials.

a. Federal Deposit Insurance Corporation Improvement Act
b. Competition law
c. Fair debt collection
d. Foreign Corrupt Practices Act

19. In finance, the value of an option consists of two components, its intrinsic value and its _____. Time value is simply the difference between option value and intrinsic value. _____ is also known as theta, extrinsic value, or instrumental value.

a. Conservatism
b. Debt buyer
c. Global Squeeze
d. Time value

20. Simply put, _____ is the value of money figuring in a given amount of interest for a given amount of time. For example 100 dollars of todays money held for a year at 5 percent interest is worth 105 dollars, therefore 100 dollars paid now or 105 dollars paid exactly one year from now is the same amount of payment of money with that given intersest at that given amount of time. This notion dates at least to Martín de Azpilcueta of the School of Salamanca.

All of the standard calculations for _____ derive from the most basic algebraic expression for the present value of a future sum, 'discounted' to the present by an amount equal to the _____. For example, a sum of FV to be received in one year is discounted (at the rate of interest r) to give a sum of PV at present: $PV = FV -- r·PV = FV/(1+r)$.

a. Zero-coupon bond
b. Current account
c. Coefficient of variation
d. Time value of money

Chapter 5. The Value of Money

1. _____ is a fee paid on borrowed assets. It is the price paid for the use of borrowed money, or, money earned by deposited funds. Assets that are sometimes lent with _____ include money, shares, consumer goods through hire purchase, major assets such as aircraft, and even entire factories in finance lease arrangements.
    a. A Random Walk Down Wall Street
    b. AAB
    c. Interest
    d. Insolvency

2. An _____ is the price a borrower pays for the use of money they do not own, and the return a lender receives for deferring the use of funds, by lending it to the borrower. _____s are normally expressed as a percentage rate over the period of one year.

    _____s targets are also a vital tool of monetary policy and are used to control variables like investment, inflation, and unemployment.

    a. ABN Amro
    b. A Random Walk Down Wall Street
    c. Interest Rate
    d. AAB

3. _____ is the concept of adding accumulated interest back to the principal, so that interest is earned on interest from that moment on. The act of declaring interest to be principal is called compounding (i.e., interest is compounded.) A loan, for example, may have its interest compounded every month: in this case, a loan with $100 principal and 1% interest per month would have a balance of $101 at the end of the first month.
    a. Risk management
    b. Penny stock
    c. 4-4-5 Calendar
    d. Compound interest

4. In finance, the value of an option consists of two components, its intrinsic value and its _____. Time value is simply the difference between option value and intrinsic value. _____ is also known as theta, extrinsic value, or instrumental value.
    a. Conservatism
    b. Global Squeeze
    c. Debt buyer
    d. Time value

5. Simply put, _____ is the value of money figuring in a given amount of interest for a given amount of time. For example 100 dollars of todays money held for a year at 5 percent interest is worth 105 dollars, therefore 100 dollars paid now or 105 dollars paid exactly one year from now is the same amount of payment of money with that given intersest at that given amount of time. This notion dates at least to Martín de Azpilcueta of the School of Salamanca.

    All of the standard calculations for _____ derive from the most basic algebraic expression for the present value of a future sum, 'discounted' to the present by an amount equal to the _____. For example, a sum of FV to be received in one year is discounted (at the rate of interest r) to give a sum of PV at present: PV = FV -- rÂ·PV = FV/(1+r).

    a. Coefficient of variation
    b. Time value of money
    c. Zero-coupon bond
    d. Current account

6. An _____ can be defined as a contract which provides an income stream in return for an initial payment.

    An immediate _____ is an _____ for which the time between the contract date and the date of the first payment is not longer than the time interval between payments. A common use for an immediate _____ is to provide a pension to a retired person or persons.

Chapter 5. The Value of Money

a. AT'T Inc.
b. Amortization
c. Annuity
d. Intrinsic value

7. _____ measures the nominal future sum of money that a given sum of money is 'worth' at a specified time in the future assuming a certain interest rate rate of return; it is the present value multiplied by the accumulation function.

The value does not include corrections for inflation or other factors that affect the true value of money in the future. This is used in time value of money calculations.

a. Present value of costs
b. Future value
c. Discounted cash flow
d. Future-oriented

8. _____ is the value on a given date of a future payment or series of future payments, discounted to reflect the time value of money and other factors such as investment risk. _____ calculations are widely used in business and economics to provide a means to compare cash flows at different times on a meaningful 'like to like' basis.

The most commonly applied model of the time value of money is compound interest.

a. Present value of benefits
b. Net present value
c. Negative gearing
d. Present value

9. _____ is the balance of the amounts of cash being received and paid by a business during a defined period of time, sometimes tied to a specific project. Measurement of _____ can be used

- to evaluate the state or performance of a business or project.
- to determine problems with liquidity. Being profitable does not necessarily mean being liquid. A company can fail because of a shortage of cash, even while profitable.
- to generate project rate of returns. The time of _____s into and out of projects are used as inputs to financial models such as internal rate of return, and net present value.
- to examine income or growth of a business when it is believed that accrual accounting concepts do not represent economic realities. Alternately, _____ can be used to 'validate' the net income generated by accrual accounting.

_____ as a generic term may be used differently depending on context, and certain _____ definitions may be adapted by analysts and users for their own uses. Common terms include operating _____ and free _____.

_____s can be classified into:

1. Operational _____s: Cash received or expended as a result of the company's core business activities.
2. Investment _____s: Cash received or expended through capital expenditure, investments or acquisitions.
3. Financing _____s: Cash received or expended as a result of financial activities, such as interests and dividends.

Chapter 5. The Value of Money 39

All three together - the net _____ - are necessary to reconcile the beginning cash balance to the ending cash balance. Loan draw downs or equity injections, that is just shifting of capital but no expenditure as such, are not considered in the net _____.

- a. Corporate finance
- b. Shareholder value
- c. Real option
- d. Cash flow

10. A '_____' is a 'Charge' that is paid to obtain the right to delay a payment. Essentially, the payer purchases the right to make a given payment in the future instead of in the Present. The '_____', or 'Charge' that must be paid to delay the payment, is simply the difference between what the payment amount would be if it were paid in the present and what the payment amount would be paid if it were paid in the future.

- a. Value at risk
- b. Risk aversion
- c. Discount
- d. Risk modeling

11. _____ is the process of decreasing an amount over a period of time. The word comes from Middle English amortisen to kill, alienate in mortmain, from Anglo-French amorteser, alteration of amortir, from Vulgar Latin admortire to kill, from Latin ad- + mort-, mors death. Particular instances of the term include:

- _____ (business), the allocation of a lump sum amount to different time periods, particularly for loans and other forms of finance, including related interest or other finance charges.
    - _____ schedule, a table detailing each periodic payment on a loan (typically a mortgage), as generated by an _____ calculator.
    - Negative _____, an _____ schedule where the loan amount actually increases through not paying the full interest
- Amortized analysis, analyzing the execution cost of algorithms over a sequence of operations.
- _____ of capital expenditures of certain assets under accounting rules, particularly intangible assets, in a manner analogous to depreciation.
- _____ (tax law)

_____ is also used in the context of zoning regulations and describes the time in which a property owner has to relocate when the property's use constitutes a preexisting nonconforming use under zoning regulations.

- Depreciation

- a. Intrinsic value
- b. Amortization
- c. Option
- d. AT'T Inc.

12. An _____ is a table detailing each periodic payment on a amortizing loan (typically a mortgage), as generated by an amortization calculator.

While a portion of every payment is applied towards both the interest and the principal balance of the loan, the exact amount applied to principal each time varies (with the remainder going to interest.) An _____ reveals the specific monetary amount put towards interest, as well as the specific put towards the Principal balance, with each payment.

Chapter 5. The Value of Money

a. Adjusted basis
b. Annual report
c. Adjusting entries
d. Amortization schedule

13. In finance and economics _____ refers to the rate of interest before adjustment for inflation (in contrast with the real interest rate); or, for interest balls stated' without adjustment for the full effect of compounding (also referred to as the nominal annual rate.) An interest rate is called nominal if the frequency of compounding (e.g. a month) is not identical to the basic time unit (normally a year.)

The real interest rate includes compensation for the lender's lost value due to inflation, whereas the _____ excludes inflation.

a. Cash accumulation equation
b. Nominal interest rate
c. Shanghai Interbank Offered Rate
d. SIBOR

14. A _____ is an annuity in which the periodic payments begin on a fixed date and continue indefinitely. It is sometimes referred to as a perpetual annuity. Fixed coupon payments on permanently invested (irredeemable) sums of money are prime examples of these. Scholarships paid perpetually from an endowment fit the definition of _____.

a. Stochastic volatility
b. Perpetuity
c. Current yield
d. LIBOR market model

15. In finance, a _____ is a debt security, in which the authorized issuer owes the holders a debt and, depending on the terms of the _____, is obliged to pay interest (the coupon) and/or to repay the principal at a later date, termed maturity.

Thus a _____ is a loan: the issuer is the borrower, the _____ holder is the lender, and the coupon is the interest. _____s provide the borrower with external funds to finance long-term investments, or, in the case of government _____s, to finance current expenditure.

a. Bond
b. Convertible bond
c. Puttable bond
d. Catastrophe bonds

16. _____ expresses an annual rate of interest taking into account the effect of compounding, usually for deposit or investment products (such as a certificate of deposit.) It is analogous to the Annual percentage rate (APR), which is used for loans. In some jurisdictions, the use and definition of _____ may be regulated by a government agency, in which case it would generally be capitalized.

a. A Random Walk Down Wall Street
b. Annual percentage yield
c. ABN Amro
d. AAB

17. The _____, effective annual interest rate, Annual Equivalent Rate (AER) or simply effective rate is the interest rate on a loan or financial product restated from the nominal interest rate as an interest rate with annual compound interest. It is used to compare the annual interest between loans with different compounding terms (daily, monthly, annually, or other.)

Chapter 5. The Value of Money

The _____ differs in two important respects from the annual percentage rate (APR):

1. the _____ generally does not incorporate one-time charges such as front-end fees;
2. the _____ is (generally) not defined by legal or regulatory authorities (as APR is in many jurisdictions.)

By contrast, the 'effective APR' is used as a legal term, where front-fees and other costs can be included, as defined by local law.

Annual Percentage Yield or effective annual yield is the analogous concept used for savings or investment products, such as a certificate of deposit.

a. A Random Walk Down Wall Street
b. AAB
c. Effective interest rate
d. ABN Amro

18. _____ or financing is to provide capital (funds), which means money for a project, a person, a business or any other private or public institutions.

Those funds can be allocated for either short term or long term purposes. The health fund is a new way of _____ private healthcare centers.

a. Product life cycle
b. Proxy fight
c. Synthetic CDO
d. Funding

19. In finance, the term _____ describes the amount in cash that returns to the owners of a security. Normally it does not include the price variations, at the difference of the total return. _____ applies to various stated rates of return on stocks (common and preferred, and convertible), fixed income instruments (bonds, notes, bills, strips, zero coupon), and some other investment type insurance products (e.g. annuities.)

a. 4-4-5 Calendar
b. Yield to maturity
c. Macaulay duration
d. Yield

Chapter 6. Risk and Rates of Return

1. The _____ is an American stock exchange. It is the largest electronic screen-based equity securities trading market in the United States. With approximately 3,200 companies, it has more trading volume per day than any other stock exchange in the world.
   - a. 4-4-5 Calendar
   - b. Nasdaq
   - c. 529 plan
   - d. 7-Eleven

2. _____ or economic opportunity loss is the value of the next best alternative foregone as the result of making a decision. _____ analysis is an important part of a company's decision-making processes but is not treated as an actual cost in any financial statement. The next best thing that a person can engage in is referred to as the _____ of doing the best thing and ignoring the next best thing to be done.
   - a. A Random Walk Down Wall Street
   - b. AAB
   - c. Opportunity cost
   - d. ABN Amro

3. In finance, _____, also known as return on investment is the ratio of money gained or lost on an investment relative to the amount of money invested. The amount of money gained or lost may be referred to as interest, profit/loss, gain/loss, or net income/loss. The money invested may be referred to as the asset, capital, principal, or the cost basis of the investment.
   - a. Composiition of Creditors
   - b. Stock or scrip dividends
   - c. Doctrine of the Proper Law
   - d. Rate of return

4. A mutual shareholder or _____ is an individual or company (including a corporation) that legally owns one or more shares of stock in a joint stock company. A company's shareholders collectively own that company. Thus, the typical goal of such companies is to enhance shareholder value.
   - a. Trading curb
   - b. Stockholder
   - c. Limit order
   - d. Stock market bubble

5. In economics, business, and accounting, a _____ is the value of money that has been used up to produce something, and hence is not available for use anymore. In business, the _____ may be one of acquisition, in which case the amount of money expended to acquire it is counted as _____. In this case, money is the input that is gone in order to acquire the thing.
   - a. Marginal cost
   - b. Fixed costs
   - c. Sliding scale fees
   - d. Cost

6. In finance, a _____ is a debt security, in which the authorized issuer owes the holders a debt and, depending on the terms of the _____, is obliged to pay interest (the coupon) and/or to repay the principal at a later date, termed maturity.

   Thus a _____ is a loan: the issuer is the borrower, the _____ holder is the lender, and the coupon is the interest. _____s provide the borrower with external funds to finance long-term investments, or, in the case of government _____s, to finance current expenditure.

   - a. Catastrophe bonds
   - b. Convertible bond
   - c. Puttable bond
   - d. Bond

7. A _____ is a bond issued by a corporation. The term is usually applied to longer-term debt instruments, generally with a maturity date falling at least a year after their issue date. (The term 'commercial paper' is sometimes used for instruments with a shorter maturity.)

Chapter 6. Risk and Rates of Return

a. Brady bonds
c. Serial bond
b. Government bond
d. Corporate bond

8. A _____ is an international bond that is denominated in a currency not native to the country where it is issued. It can be categorised according to the currency in which it is issued. London is one of the centers of the _____ market, but _____ s may be traded throughout the world - for example in Singapore or Tokyo.
   a. Eurobond
   c. Education production function
   b. Interest rate option
   d. Economic entity

9. A _____ is a bond issued by a national government denominated in the country's own currency. Bonds issued by national governments in foreign currencies are normally referred to as sovereign bonds. The first ever _____ was issued by the British government in 1693 to raise money to fund a war against France.
   a. Zero-coupon bond
   c. Government bond
   b. Municipal bond
   d. Collateralized debt obligations

10. In economic models, the _____ time frame assumes no fixed factors of production. Firms can enter or leave the marketplace, and the cost (and availability) of land, labor, raw materials, and capital goods can be assumed to vary. In contrast, in the short-run time frame, certain factors are assumed to be fixed, because there is not sufficient time for them to change.
    a. 4-4-5 Calendar
    c. Short-run
    b. 529 plan
    d. Long-run

11.

In finance, the _____ can be the expected rate of return above the risk-free interest rate. When measuring risk, a common sense approach is to compare the risk-free return on T-bills and the very risky return on other investments. The difference between these two returns can be interpreted as a measure of the excess return on the average risky asset. This excess return is known as the _____.

   a. Risk adjusted return on capital
   c. Risk aversion
   b. Risk modeling
   d. Risk premium

12. _____ mature in one year or less. Like zero-coupon bonds, they do not pay interest prior to maturity; instead they are sold at a discount of the par value to create a positive yield to maturity. Many regard _____ as the least risky investment available to U.S. investors.
    a. 4-4-5 Calendar
    c. Treasury securities
    b. Treasury Inflation Protected Securities
    d. Treasury bills

13. A _____ is an exchange of promises between two or more parties to do an act which is enforceable in a court of law. It is where an unqualified offer meets a qualified acceptance and the parties reach Consensus ad Idem. The parties must have the necessary capacity to _____ and the _____ must not be either trifling, indeterminate, impossible or illegal.
    a. 4-4-5 Calendar
    c. 7-Eleven
    b. 529 plan
    d. Contract

14. In business and finance, a _____ (also referred to as equity _____) of stock means a _____ of ownership in a corporation (company.) In the plural, stocks is often used as a synonym for _____s especially in the United States, but it is less commonly used that way outside of North America.

In the United Kingdom, South Africa, and Australia, stock can also refer to completely different financial instruments such as government bonds or, less commonly, to all kinds of marketable securities.

    a. Procter ' Gamble   b. Bucket shop
    c. Margin   d. Share

15. In economics, the _____ is the proposition by Irving Fisher that the real interest rate is independent of monetary measures, especially the nominal interest rate. The Fisher equation is

$r_r = r_n >- >\pi^e$.

This means, the real interest rate (r_r) equals the nominal interest rate (r_n) minus expected rate of inflation ($>\pi^e$.) Here all the rates are continuously compounded.

    a. 529 plan   b. 4-4-5 Calendar
    c. 7-Eleven   d. Fisher hypothesis

16. In economics, _____ is a rise in the general level of prices of goods and services in an economy over a period of time. The term '_____' once referred to increases in the money supply (monetary _____); however, economic debates about the relationship between money supply and price levels have led to its primary use today in describing price _____.
_____ can also be described as a decline in the real value of money--a loss of purchasing power in the medium of exchange which is also the monetary unit of account.

    a. A Random Walk Down Wall Street   b. AAB
    c. Inflation   d. ABN Amro

17. _____ is a fee paid on borrowed assets. It is the price paid for the use of borrowed money , or, money earned by deposited funds . Assets that are sometimes lent with _____ include money, shares, consumer goods through hire purchase, major assets such as aircraft, and even entire factories in finance lease arrangements.
    a. Interest   b. AAB
    c. Insolvency   d. A Random Walk Down Wall Street

18. An _____ is the price a borrower pays for the use of money they do not own, and the return a lender receives for deferring the use of funds, by lending it to the borrower. _____s are normally expressed as a percentage rate over the period of one year.

_____s targets are also a vital tool of monetary policy and are used to control variables like investment, inflation, and unemployment.

    a. A Random Walk Down Wall Street   b. Interest rate
    c. ABN Amro   d. AAB

Chapter 6. Risk and Rates of Return

19. In finance and economics _____ refers to the rate of interest before adjustment for inflation (in contrast with the real interest rate); or, for interest balls stated' without adjustment for the full effect of compounding (also referred to as the nominal annual rate.) An interest rate is called nominal if the frequency of compounding (e.g. a month) is not identical to the basic time unit (normally a year.)

The real interest rate includes compensation for the lender's lost value due to inflation, whereas the _____ excludes inflation.

    a. Cash accumulation equation   b. Shanghai Interbank Offered Rate
    c. SIBOR   d. Nominal interest rate

20. The '_____' is approximately the nominal interest rate minus the inflation rate Since the inflation rate over the course of a loan is not known initially, volatility in inflation represents a risk to both the lender and the borrower.

In economics and finance, an individual who lends money for repayment at a later point in time expects to be compensated for the time value of money, or not having the use of that money while it is lent.

    a. 4-4-5 Calendar   b. 7-Eleven
    c. 529 plan   d. Real Interest rate

21. In finance, the yield curve is the relation between the interest rate (or cost of borrowing) and the time to maturity of the debt for a given borrower in a given currency. For example, the current U.S. dollar interest rates paid on U.S. Treasury securities for various maturities are closely watched by many traders, and are commonly plotted on a graph such as the one on the right which is informally called 'the yield curve.' More formal mathematical descriptions of this relation are often called the _____.

The yield of a debt instrument is the annualized percentage increase in the value of the investment.

    a. Term structure of interest rates   b. 4-4-5 Calendar
    c. 7-Eleven   d. 529 plan

22. In finance, the term _____ describes the amount in cash that returns to the owners of a security. Normally it does not include the price variations, at the difference of the total return. _____ applies to various stated rates of return on stocks (common and preferred, and convertible), fixed income instruments (bonds, notes, bills, strips, zero coupon), and some other investment type insurance products (e.g. annuities.)

    a. Macaulay duration   b. Yield to maturity
    c. 4-4-5 Calendar   d. Yield

23. The _____ or redemption yield is the yield promised to the bondholder on the assumption that the bond or other fixed-interest security such as gilts will be held to maturity, that all coupon and principal payments will be made and coupon payments are reinvested at the bond's promised yield at the same rate as invested. It is a measure of the return of the bond. This technique in theory allows investors to calculate the fair value of different financial instruments.

    a. 4-4-5 Calendar   b. Yield to maturity
    c. Yield   d. Macaulay duration

Chapter 6. Risk and Rates of Return

24. _____ is a life of security. It may also refer to the final payment date of a loan or other financial instrument, at which point all remaining interest and principal is due to be paid.

1, 3, 6 months _____ band can be calculated by using 30-day per month periods.

   a. Replacement cost   b. Maturity
   c. Primary market   d. False billing

25. A _____ is a fungible, negotiable instrument representing financial value. They are broadly categorized into debt securities (such as banknotes, bonds and debentures), and equity securities; e.g., common stocks. The company or other entity issuing the _____ is called the issuer.

   a. Tracking stock   b. Book entry
   c. Securities lending   d. Security

26. In probability and statistics, the _____ of a collection of numbers is a measure of the dispersion of the numbers from their expected (mean) value. It can apply to a probability distribution, a random variable, a population or a data set. The _____ is usually denoted with the letter σ (lowercase sigma.)

   a. Kurtosis   b. Sample size
   c. Mean   d. Standard deviation

27. _____ in finance is a risk management technique, related to hedging, that mixes a wide variety of investments within a portfolio. Because the fluctuations of a single security have less impact on a diverse portfolio, _____ minimizes the risk from any one investment.

A simple example of _____ is the following: On a particular island the entire economy consists of two companies: one that sells umbrellas and another that sells sunscreen.

   a. 4-4-5 Calendar   b. 7-Eleven
   c. 529 plan   d. Diversification

28. In finance, _____ is that risk which is common to an entire market and not to any individual entity or component thereof. It should be distinguished from systemic risk which is the risk that the entire financial system will collapse as a result of some catastrophic event.

Risks can be reduced in four main ways: Avoidance, Reduction, Retention and Transfer.

   a. Conglomerate merger   b. Capital surplus
   c. Primary market   d. Systematic risk

29. In business and accounting, _____s are everything of value that is owned by a person or company. The balance sheet of a firm records the monetary value of the _____s owned by the firm. The two major _____ classes are tangible _____s and intangible _____s.

   a. EBITDA   b. Asset
   c. Accounts payable   d. Income

Chapter 6. Risk and Rates of Return

30. _____ is a term used to refer to how an investor distributes his or her investments among various classes of investment vehicles (e.g., stocks and bonds.)

A large part of financial planning is finding an _____ that is appropriate for a given person in terms of their appetite for and ability to shoulder risk. This can depend on various factors; see investor profile.

a. Investing online
b. Alternative investment
c. Investment performance
d. Asset allocation

31. A _____, is a mathematical formalization of a trajectory that consists of taking successive random steps. The results of _____ analysis have been applied to computer science, physics, ecology, economics and a number of other fields as a fundamental model for random processes in time. For example, the path traced by a molecule as it travels in a liquid or a gas, the search path of a foraging animal, the price of a fluctuating stock and the financial status of a gambler can all be modeled as _____s.

a. Random Walk
b. 7-Eleven
c. 4-4-5 Calendar
d. 529 plan

32. In finance, the _____ is used to determine a theoretically appropriate required rate of return of an asset, if that asset is to be added to an already well-diversified portfolio, given that asset's non-diversifiable risk. The model takes into account the asset's sensitivity to non-diversifiable risk (also known as systemic risk or market risk), often represented by the quantity beta (β) in the financial industry, as well as the expected return of the market and the expected return of a theoretical risk-free asset.

The model was introduced by Jack Treynor (1961, 1962), William Sharpe (1964), John Lintner (1965a,b) and Jan Mossin (1966) independently, building on the earlier work of Harry Markowitz on diversification and modern portfolio theory.

a. Hull-White model
b. Random walk hypothesis
c. Cox-Ingersoll-Ross model
d. Capital asset pricing model

48 **Chapter 6. Risk and Rates of Return**

33. The term _____ has three unrelated technical definitions, and is also used in a variety of non-technical ways.

- In financial economics, it refers to any asset used to make money, as opposed to assets used for personal enjoyment or consumption. This is an important distinction because two people can disagree sharply about the value of personal assets, one person might think a sports car is more valuable than a pickup truck, another person might have the opposite taste. But if an asset is held for the purpose of making money, taste has nothing to do with it, only differences of opinion about how much money the asset will produce. With the further assumption that people agree on the probability distribution of future cash flows, it is possible to have an objective _____ pricing model. Even without the assumption of agreement, it is possible to set rational limits on _____ value.
- In governmental accounting, it is defined as any asset used in operations with an initial useful life extending beyond one reporting period. Generally, government managers have a 'stewardship' duty to maintain _____s under their control. See International Public Sector Accounting Standards for details.
- In US tax accounting, it is defined as any property other than a list of exceptions. The main exceptions are anything held for sale, and any real estate or depreciable property used in business. Almost everything you own and use for personal purposes, pleasure or investment is a _____. If something is a _____ for tax purposes, gains or losses on sale or disposition are capital gains or capital losses. For individuals, however, capital losses on property held for personal use are generally not deductible. See the IRS publication Tax Facts about Capital Gains and Losses for details.

A well-known financial accounting textbook advises that the term be avoided except in tax accounting because it is used in so many different senses, not all of them well-defined. For example it is often used as a synonym for fixed assets or for investments in securities.

A common non-technical usage occurs when people ask that employees or the environment or something else be treated as a _____.

a. Capital asset
c. Political risk
b. Solvency
d. Settlement date

34. In Modern Portfolio Theory, the _____ is the graphical representation of the Capital Asset Pricing Model. It displays the expected rate of return for an overall market as a function of systematic (non-diversifiable) risk (beta.)

The Y-Intercept (beta=0) of the _____ is equal to the risk-free interest rate.

a. Security market line
c. Rebalancing
b. Certificate in Investment Performance Measurement
d. Divestment

35. In finance, _____ is the process of estimating the potential market value of a financial asset or liability. they can be done on assets (for example, investments in marketable securities such as stocks, options, business enterprises, or intangible assets such as patents and trademarks) or on liabilities (e.g., Bonds issued by a company.) _____s are required in many contexts including investment analysis, capital budgeting, merger and acquisition transactions, financial reporting, taxable events to determine the proper tax liability, and in litigation.

a. Margin
c. Share
b. Procter ' Gamble
d. Valuation

Chapter 7. Valuation and Characteristics of Bonds

1. In finance, a _____ is a debt security, in which the authorized issuer owes the holders a debt and, depending on the terms of the _____, is obliged to pay interest (the coupon) and/or to repay the principal at a later date, termed maturity.

   Thus a _____ is a loan: the issuer is the borrower, the _____ holder is the lender, and the coupon is the interest. _____s provide the borrower with external funds to finance long-term investments, or, in the case of government _____s, to finance current expenditure.

   a. Catastrophe bonds
   b. Bond
   c. Puttable bond
   d. Convertible bond

2. A _____ is defined as a certificate of agreement of loans which is given under the company's stamp and carries an undertaking that the _____ holder will get a fixed return (fixed on the basis of interest rates) and the principal amount whenever the _____ matures.

   In finance, a _____ is a long-term debt instrument used by governments and large companies to obtain funds. It is defined as 'a debt secured only by the debtor's earning power, not by a lien on any specific asset.' It is similar to a bond except the securitization conditions are different.

   a. Partial Payment
   b. Collection agency
   c. Collateral Management
   d. Debenture

3. A _____ is an international bond that is denominated in a currency not native to the country where it is issued. It can be categorised according to the currency in which it is issued. London is one of the centers of the _____ market, but _____s may be traded throughout the world - for example in Singapore or Tokyo.

   a. Interest rate option
   b. Economic entity
   c. Education production function
   d. Eurobond

4. In finance, a _____ (non-investment grade bond, speculative grade bond or junk bond) is a bond that is rated below investment grade at the time of purchase. These bonds have a higher risk of default or other adverse credit events, but typically pay higher yields than better quality bonds in order to make them attractive to investors.

   a. Sharpe ratio
   b. Private equity
   c. Volatility
   d. High yield bond

5. The coupon or _____ of a bond is the amount of interest paid per year expressed as a percentage of the face value of the bond.

   For example if you hold $10,000 nominal of a bond described as a 4.5% loan stock, you will receive $450 in interest each year (probably in two installments of $225 each.)

   Not all bonds have coupons.

   a. Zero-coupon bond
   b. Puttable bond
   c. Revenue bonds
   d. Coupon rate

Chapter 7. Valuation and Characteristics of Bonds

6. In business and accounting, _____s are everything of value that is owned by a person or company. The balance sheet of a firm records the monetary value of the _____s owned by the firm. The two major _____ classes are tangible _____s and intangible _____s.

   a. Accounts payable
   b. EBITDA
   c. Income
   d. Asset

7. _____, refers to consumption opportunity gained by an entity within a specified time frame, which is generally expressed in monetary terms. However, for households and individuals, '_____ is the sum of all the wages, salaries, profits, interests payments, rents and other forms of earnings received... in a given period of time.' For firms, _____ generally refers to net-profit: what remains of revenue after expenses have been subtracted.

   a. Accrual
   b. Income
   c. OIBDA
   d. Annual report

8. _____ is a fee paid on borrowed assets. It is the price paid for the use of borrowed money, or, money earned by deposited funds. Assets that are sometimes lent with _____ include money, shares, consumer goods through hire purchase, major assets such as aircraft, and even entire factories in finance lease arrangements.

   a. Interest
   b. AAB
   c. Insolvency
   d. A Random Walk Down Wall Street

9. An _____ is the price a borrower pays for the use of money they do not own, and the return a lender receives for deferring the use of funds, by lending it to the borrower. _____s are normally expressed as a percentage rate over the period of one year.

   _____s targets are also a vital tool of monetary policy and are used to control variables like investment, inflation, and unemployment.

   a. ABN Amro
   b. AAB
   c. A Random Walk Down Wall Street
   d. Interest rate

10. _____ is a life of security. It may also refer to the final payment date of a loan or other financial instrument, at which point all remaining interest and principal is due to be paid.

    1, 3, 6 months _____ band can be calculated by using 30-day per month periods.

    a. Maturity
    b. False billing
    c. Primary market
    d. Replacement cost

11. _____, in finance and accounting, means stated value or face value. From this comes the expressions at par (at the _____), over par (over _____) and under par (under _____.)

    The term '_____' has several meanings depending on context and geography.

    a. FIDC
    b. Global Squeeze
    c. Sinking fund
    d. Par value

Chapter 7. Valuation and Characteristics of Bonds

12. The _____, interest yield, income yield, flat yield or running yield is a financial term used in reference to bonds and other fixed-interest securities such as gilts. It is the ratio of the annual interest payment and the bond's current price.

The _____ only therefore refers to the yield of the bond at the current moment. It does not reflect the total return over the life of the bond. In particular, it takes no account of reinvestment risk (the uncertainty about the rate at which future cashflows can be reinvested) or the fact that bonds usually mature at par value, which can be an important component of a bond's return.

   a. Modified Internal Rate of Return
   b. Stochastic volatility
   c. Perpetuity
   d. Current yield

13. In finance, the term _____ describes the amount in cash that returns to the owners of a security. Normally it does not include the price variations, at the difference of the total return. _____ applies to various stated rates of return on stocks (common and preferred, and convertible), fixed income instruments (bonds, notes, bills, strips, zero coupon), and some other investment type insurance products (e.g. annuities.)
   a. Yield to maturity
   b. Yield
   c. Macaulay duration
   d. 4-4-5 Calendar

14. A _____ is a bond issued by a corporation. The term is usually applied to longer-term debt instruments, generally with a maturity date falling at least a year after their issue date. (The term 'commercial paper' is sometimes used for instruments with a shorter maturity.)
   a. Corporate bond
   b. Brady bonds
   c. Government bond
   d. Serial bond

15. Behavioral economics and _____ are closely related fields that have evolved to be a separate branch of economic and financial analysis which applies scientific research on human and social, cognitive and emotional factors to better understand economic decisions by, say, consumers, borrowers, investors, and how they affect market prices, returns and the allocation of resources.

The field is primarily concerned with the bounds of rationality (selfishness, self-control) of economic agents. Behavioral models typically integrate insights from psychology with neo-classical economic theory.

   a. Medium of exchange
   b. Recession
   c. Market structure
   d. Behavioral finance

16. _____, also called fair price (in a commonplace conflation of the two distinct concepts), is a concept used in finance and economics, defined as a rational and unbiased estimate of the potential market price of a good, service, or asset, taking into account such objective factors as:

   - acquisition/production/distribution costs, replacement costs, or costs of close substitutes
   - actual utility at a given level of development of social productive capability
   - supply vs. demand

Chapter 7. Valuation and Characteristics of Bonds

and subjective factors such as

- risk characteristics
- cost of capital
- individually perceived utility

In accounting, _____ is used as an estimate of the market value of an asset (or liability) for which a market price cannot be determined (usually because there is no established market for the asset.) Under GAAP (FAS 157), _____ is the amount at which the asset could be bought or sold in a current transaction between willing parties, or transferred to an equivalent party, other than in a liquidation sale. This is used for assets whose carrying value is based on mark-to-market valuations; for assets carried at historical cost, the _____ of the asset is not used. One example of where _____ is an issue is a College kitchen with a cost of $2 million which was built 5 years ago.

a. 4-4-5 Calendar
c. 7-Eleven
b. Fair value
d. 529 plan

17. In finance, _____ refers to the value of a security which is intrinsic to or contained in the security itself. It is also frequently called fundamental value. It is ordinarily calculated by summing the future income generated by the asset, and discounting it to the present value.

a. Intrinsic value
c. Amortization
b. Alpha
d. Accretion

18. In law, _____ refers to the process by which a company (or part of a company) is brought to an end, and the assets and property of the company redistributed. _____ can also be referred to as winding-up or dissolution, although dissolution technically refers to the last stage of _____. The process of _____ also arises when customs, an authority or agency in a country responsible for collecting and safeguarding customs duties, determines the final computation or ascertainment of the duties or drawback accruing on an entry.

a. 4-4-5 Calendar
c. Debt settlement
b. 529 plan
d. Liquidation

19. _____ is the likely price of an asset when it is allowed insufficient time to sell on the open market, thereby reducing its exposure to potential buyers. _____ is typically lower than fair market value. Unlike cash or securities, certain illiquid assets, like real estate, often require a period of several months in order to obtain their fair market value in a sale, and will generally sell for a significantly lower price if a sale is forced to occur in a shorter time period.

a. Real estate investing
c. REIT
b. Tenancy
d. Liquidation value

20. _____ is the price at which an asset would trade in a competitive Walrasian auction setting. _____ is often used interchangeably with open _____, fair value or fair _____, although these terms have distinct definitions in different standards, and may differ in some circumstances.

International Valuation Standards defines _____ as 'the estimated amount for which a property should exchange on the date of valuation between a willing buyer and a willing seller in an arm'e;s-length transaction after proper marketing wherein the parties had each acted knowledgeably, prudently, and without compulsion.'

Chapter 7. Valuation and Characteristics of Bonds 53

_____ is a concept distinct from market price, which is 'e;the price at which one can transact'e;, while _____ is 'e;the true underlying value'e; according to theoretical standards.

a. Wrap account
c. Debt restructuring
b. T-Model
d. Market value

21. An _____ or index tracker is a collective investment scheme (usually a mutual fund or exchange-traded fund) that aims to replicate the movements of an index of a specific financial market regardless of market conditions.

Tracking can be achieved by trying to hold all of the securities in the index, in the same proportions as the index. Other methods include statistically sampling the market and holding 'representative' securities.

a. Investment company
c. A Random Walk Down Wall Street
b. AAB
d. Index fund

22. A _____ is a private or public market for the trading of company stock and derivatives of company stock at an agreed price; these are securities listed on a stock exchange as well as those only traded privately.

The size of the world _____ is estimated at about $36.6 trillion US at the beginning of October 2008 . The world derivatives market has been estimated at about $480 trillion face or nominal value, 12 times the size of the entire world economy.

a. Anton Gelonkin
c. Adolph Coors
b. Andrew Tobias
d. Stock market

23. A _____ is a type of economic bubble taking place in stock markets when price of stocks rise and become overvalued by any measure of stock valuation.

The existence of _____s is at odds with the assumptions of efficient market theory which assumes rational investor behaviour. Behavioral finance theory attribute _____s to cognitive biases that lead to groupthink and herd behavior.

a. Stock market bubble
c. Stockholder
b. Stock split
d. Trading curb

24. _____ or economic opportunity loss is the value of the next best alternative foregone as the result of making a decision. _____ analysis is an important part of a company's decision-making processes but is not treated as an actual cost in any financial statement. The next best thing that a person can engage in is referred to as the _____ of doing the best thing and ignoring the next best thing to be done.

a. ABN Amro
c. Opportunity cost
b. AAB
d. A Random Walk Down Wall Street

Chapter 7. Valuation and Characteristics of Bonds

25. In economics, business, and accounting, a _____ is the value of money that has been used up to produce something, and hence is not available for use anymore. In business, the _____ may be one of acquisition, in which case the amount of money expended to acquire it is counted as _____. In this case, money is the input that is gone in order to acquire the thing.
   a. Sliding scale fees
   b. Marginal cost
   c. Fixed costs
   d. Cost

26. In finance, _____ is the process of estimating the potential market value of a financial asset or liability. they can be done on assets (for example, investments in marketable securities such as stocks, options, business enterprises, or intangible assets such as patents and trademarks) or on liabilities (e.g., Bonds issued by a company.) _____s are required in many contexts including investment analysis, capital budgeting, merger and acquisition transactions, financial reporting, taxable events to determine the proper tax liability, and in litigation.
   a. Procter ' Gamble
   b. Share
   c. Margin
   d. Valuation

27. _____ is the process of determining the fair price of a bond. As with any security or capital investment, the fair value of a bond is the present value of the stream of cash flows it is expected to generate. Hence, the price or value of a bond is determined by discounting the bond's expected cash flows to the present using the appropriate discount rate.
   a. Bond fund
   b. Catastrophe bonds
   c. Bond valuation
   d. Collateralized debt obligations

28. In finance, _____, also known as return on investment is the ratio of money gained or lost on an investment relative to the amount of money invested. The amount of money gained or lost may be referred to as interest, profit/loss, gain/loss, or net income/loss. The money invested may be referred to as the asset, capital, principal, or the cost basis of the investment.
   a. Stock or scrip dividends
   b. Rate of return
   c. Composiition of Creditors
   d. Doctrine of the Proper Law

29. The _____ or redemption yield is the yield promised to the bondholder on the assumption that the bond or other fixed-interest security such as gilts will be held to maturity, that all coupon and principal payments will be made and coupon payments are reinvested at the bond's promised yield at the same rate as invested. It is a measure of the return of the bond. This technique in theory allows investors to calculate the fair value of different financial instruments.
   a. Yield
   b. 4-4-5 Calendar
   c. Macaulay duration
   d. Yield to maturity

30. A '_____' is a 'Charge' that is paid to obtain the right to delay a payment. Essentially, the payer purchases the right to make a given payment in the future instead of in the Present. The '_____', or 'Charge' that must be paid to delay the payment, is simply the difference between what the payment amount would be if it were paid in the present and what the payment amount would be paid if it were paid in the future.
   a. Value at risk
   b. Risk aversion
   c. Risk modeling
   d. Discount

31. A _____ is a bond bought at a price lower than its face value, with the face value repaid at the time of maturity. It does not make periodic interest payments, or so-called 'coupons,' hence the term zero-coupon bond. Investors earn return from the compounded interest all paid at maturity plus the difference between the discounted price of the bond and its par value.

a. Zero coupon bond
b. Bowie bonds
c. Municipal bond
d. Callable bond

32. _____ is the risk (variability in value) borne by an interest-bearing asset, such as a loan or a bond, due to variability of interest rates. In general, as rates rise, the price of a fixed rate bond will fall, and vice versa. _____ is commonly measured by the bond's duration.
   a. Official bank rate
   b. Interest rate risk
   c. A Random Walk Down Wall Street
   d. International Fisher effect

33. In economic models, the _____ time frame assumes no fixed factors of production. Firms can enter or leave the marketplace, and the cost (and availability) of land, labor, raw materials, and capital goods can be assumed to vary. In contrast, in the short-run time frame, certain factors are assumed to be fixed, because there is not sufficient time for them to change.
   a. Short-run
   b. Long-run
   c. 529 plan
   d. 4-4-5 Calendar

34. A _____ is a generic term for any bond selling for more than 100% of par value, i.e., at a price greater than 100.00, which typically occurs for high coupon bonds in a falling interest rate climate.
   a. Revenue bonds
   b. Municipal bond
   c. Nominal yield
   d. Premium bond

35. In finance, the _____ of a financial asset measures the sensitivity of the asset's price to interest rate movements, expressed as a number of years. The reason for expressing this sensitivity in years is that the time that will elapse until a cash flow is received allows more interest to accumulate. Therefore the price of an asset with long term cashflows has more interest rate sensitivity than an asset with cashflows in the near future.
   a. 4-4-5 Calendar
   b. Yield to maturity
   c. Macaulay duration
   d. Duration

Chapter 8. Stock Valuation

1. _____ is typically a higher ranking stock than voting shares, and its terms are negotiated between the corporation and the investor.

   _____ usually carry no voting rights, but may carry superior priority over common stock in the payment of dividends and upon liquidation. _____ may carry a dividend that is paid out prior to any dividends to common stock holders.

   a. Follow-on offering
   b. Preferred stock
   c. Trade-off theory
   d. Second lien loan

2. In business and accounting, _____s are everything of value that is owned by a person or company. The balance sheet of a firm records the monetary value of the _____s owned by the firm. The two major _____ classes are tangible _____s and intangible _____s.
   a. Income
   b. EBITDA
   c. Accounts payable
   d. Asset

3. _____, refers to consumption opportunity gained by an entity within a specified time frame, which is generally expressed in monetary terms. However, for households and individuals, '_____ is the sum of all the wages, salaries, profits, interests payments, rents and other forms of earnings received... in a given period of time.' For firms, _____ generally refers to net-profit: what remains of revenue after expenses have been subtracted.
   a. Annual report
   b. OIBDA
   c. Accrual
   d. Income

4. In financial accounting, _____s are precautions for which the amount or probability of occurrence are not known. Typical examples are _____s for warranty costs and _____ for taxes the term reserve is used instead of term _____; such a use, however, is inconsistent with the terminology suggested by International Accounting Standards Board.
   a. Money measurement concept
   b. Provision
   c. Momentum Accounting and Triple-Entry Bookkeeping
   d. Petty cash

5. In finance, a _____ is a type of bond that can be converted into shares of stock in the issuing company, usually at some pre-announced ratio. It is a hybrid security with debt- and equity-like features. Although it typically has a low coupon rate, the holder is compensated with the ability to convert the bond to common stock, usually at a substantial discount to the stock's market value.
   a. Corporate bond
   b. Convertible bond
   c. Bond fund
   d. Gilts

6. In business and finance, a _____ (also referred to as equity _____) of stock means a _____ of ownership in a corporation (company.) In the plural, stocks is often used as a synonym for _____s especially in the United States, but it is less commonly used that way outside of North America.

In the United Kingdom, South Africa, and Australia, stock can also refer to completely different financial instruments such as government bonds or, less commonly, to all kinds of marketable securities.

Chapter 8. Stock Valuation

a. Bucket shop
b. Procter ' Gamble
c. Share
d. Margin

7. A _____ is a payment made by a corporation to its shareholder members. When a corporation earns a profit or surplus, that money can be put to two uses: it can either be re-invested in the business (called retained earnings), or it can be paid to the shareholders as a _____. Many corporations retain a portion of their earnings and pay the remainder as a _____.

a. Special dividend
b. Dividend puzzle
c. Dividend yield
d. Dividend

8. _____ is capital stock which provides a specific dividend that is paid before any dividends are paid to common stock holders, and which takes precedence over common stock in the event of a liquidation. This form of financing is used by private equity investors and venture capital firms. Holders of _____ get both their money back (with interest) and the money that is distributable with respect to the percentage of common shares into which their preferred stock can convert.

a. Preferred stock
b. Cash is king
c. Shareholder value
d. Participating preferred stock

9. In finance, a _____ is a debt security, in which the authorized issuer owes the holders a debt and, depending on the terms of the _____, is obliged to pay interest (the coupon) and/or to repay the principal at a later date, termed maturity.

Thus a _____ is a loan: the issuer is the borrower, the _____ holder is the lender, and the coupon is the interest. _____s provide the borrower with external funds to finance long-term investments, or, in the case of government _____s, to finance current expenditure.

a. Catastrophe bonds
b. Puttable bond
c. Convertible bond
d. Bond

10. _____ is the quality of paper money substitutes which entitles the holder to redeem them on demand into money proper.

Historically, the banknote has followed a common or very similar pattern in the western nations. Originally decentralized and issued from various independent banks, it was gradually brought under state control and became a monopoly privilege of the central banks.

a. Devaluation
b. Petrodollar recycling
c. Functional currency
d. Convertibility

11. In finance, 'participation' is an ownership interest in a mortgage or other loan. In particular, _____ is a cooperation of multiple lenders to issue a loan (known as participation loan) to one borrower. This is usually done in order to reduce individual risks of the lenders.

a. Short positions
b. Loan participation
c. Doctrine of the Proper Law
d. Securitization

12. A _____ is a fund established by a government agency or business for the purpose of reducing debt.

Chapter 8. Stock Valuation

The _____ was first used in Great Britain in the 18th century to reduce national debt. While used by Robert Walpole in 1716 and effectively in the 1720s and early 1730s, it originated in the commercial tax syndicates of the Italian peninsula of the 14th century to retire redeemable public debt of those cities.

    a. Sinking fund   b. Modern portfolio theory
    c. Security interest   d. Debtor

13. _____ is a form of corporation equity ownership represented in the securities. It is dangerous in comparison to preferred shares and some other investment options, in that in the event of bankruptcy, _____ investors receive their funds after preferred stockholders, bondholders, creditors, etc. On the other hand, common shares on average perform better than preferred shares or bonds over time.

    a. Common stock   b. Stock market bubble
    c. Stop-limit order   d. Stock split

14. A _____ is a company that owns other companies' outstanding stock. It usually refers to a company which does not produce goods or services itself, rather its only purpose is owning shares of other companies. They allow the reduction of risk for the owners and can allow the ownership and control of a number of different companies.

    a. Federal National Mortgage Association   b. MRU Holdings
    c. Privately held company   d. Holding Company

15. The _____ of 1935 was a law that was passed by the United States Congress to facilitate regulation of electric utilities, by either limiting their operations to a single state, and thus subjecting them to effective state regulation, or forcing divestitures so that each became a single integrated system serving a limited geographic area. Another purpose of _____ was to keep utility holding companies engaged in regulated businesses from engaging in unregulated businesses. _____ required that Securities and Exchange Commission (SEC) approval be obtained by a holding company prior to engaging in a non-utility business and that such businesses be kept separate from the regulated business(es.)

    a. 529 plan   b. Garn-St. Germain Depository Institutions Act
    c. 4-4-5 Calendar   d. Public Utility Holding Company Act

16. In economics, _____ is a measure of the relative satisfaction from or desirability of consumption of various goods and services. Given this measure, one may speak meaningfully of increasing or decreasing _____, and thereby explain economic behavior in terms of attempts to increase one's _____. For illustrative purposes, changes in _____ are sometimes expressed in units called utils.

    a. AAB   b. Utility function
    c. A Random Walk Down Wall Street   d. Utility

17. A _____ is an event that may occur when a corporation's stockholders develop opposition to some aspect of the corporate governance, often focusing on directorial and management positions. Corporate activists may attempt to persuade shareholders to use their proxy votes (i.e. votes by one individual or institution as the authorized representative of another) to install new management for any of a variety of reasons.

In a _____, incumbent directors and management have the odds stacked in their favor over those trying to force the corporate change.

Chapter 8. Stock Valuation

a. Procurement
b. Forfaiting
c. Trade finance
d. Proxy fight

18. _____ is a multiple-winner voting system intended to promote proportional representation while also being simple to understand.

_____ is used frequently in corporate governance, where it is mandated by many U.S. states, and it was used to elect the Illinois House of Representatives from 1870 until its repeal in 1980. It was used in England in the late 19th century to elect school boards.

a. 4-4-5 Calendar
b. 529 plan
c. 7-Eleven
d. Cumulative voting

19. A _____ is a right to acquire certain property in preference to any other person. It usually refers to property newly coming into existence. A right to acquire existing property in preference to any other person is usually referred to as a right of first refusal.

In practice, the most common form of _____ is the right of existing shareholders to acquire newly issued shares issued by a company in a rights issue, a usually but not always public offering.

a. Court of Audit of Belgium
b. Down payment
c. Fraud deterrence
d. Pre-emption right

20. _____ is the trading of a corporation's stock or other securities (e.g. bonds or stock options) by individuals with potential access to non-public information about the company. In most countries, trading by corporate insiders such as officers, key employees, directors, and large shareholders may be legal, if this trading is done in a way that does not take advantage of non-public information. However, the term is frequently used to refer to a practice in which an insider or a related party trades based on material non-public information obtained during the performance of the insider's duties at the corporation, or otherwise in breach of a fiduciary duty or other relationship of trust and confidence or where the non-public information was misappropriated from the company.

a. Intellidex
b. Insider trading
c. Open outcry
d. Equity investment

21. _____ is a concept whereby a person's financial liability is limited to a fixed sum, most commonly the value of a person's investment in a company or partnership with _____. A shareholder in a limited company is not personally liable for any of the debts of the company, other than for the value of his investment in that company. The same is true for the members of a _____ partnership and the limited partners in a limited partnership.

a. Beneficial owner
b. Personal property
c. Sarbanes-Oxley Act
d. Limited liability

22. In finance, _____ is the process of estimating the potential market value of a financial asset or liability. they can be done on assets (for example, investments in marketable securities such as stocks, options, business enterprises, or intangible assets such as patents and trademarks) or on liabilities (e.g., Bonds issued by a company.) _____s are required in many contexts including investment analysis, capital budgeting, merger and acquisition transactions, financial reporting, taxable events to determine the proper tax liability, and in litigation.

Chapter 8. Stock Valuation

a. Share
b. Margin
c. Procter ' Gamble
d. Valuation

23. In the most general sense, a _____ is anything that is a hindrance, or puts individuals at a disadvantage.

Before we discuss the financial terms, we should note that a _____ can also have a much more important slang meaning.

This is best described in an example.

a. Limited liability
b. Liability
c. Covenant
d. McFadden Act

24. _____ is an estimate of the fair value of corporations and their stocks, by using fundamental economic criteria. This theoretical valuation has to be perfected with market criteria, as the final purpose is to determine potential market prices.

a. 4-4-5 Calendar
b. Stock Valuation
c. Security Analysis
d. Growth stocks

25. A mutual shareholder or _____ is an individual or company (including a corporation) that legally owns one or more shares of stock in a joint stock company. A company's shareholders collectively own that company. Thus, the typical goal of such companies is to enhance shareholder value.

a. Stock market bubble
b. Trading curb
c. Limit order
d. Stockholder

26. In finance, _____, also known as return on investment is the ratio of money gained or lost on an investment relative to the amount of money invested. The amount of money gained or lost may be referred to as interest, profit/loss, gain/loss, or net income/loss. The money invested may be referred to as the asset, capital, principal, or the cost basis of the investment.

a. Doctrine of the Proper Law
b. Composiition of Creditors
c. Rate of return
d. Stock or scrip dividends

27. _____ is a business buzz term, which implies that the ultimate measure of a company's success is to enrich shareholders. It became popular during the 1980s, and is particularly associated with former CEO of General Electric, Jack Welch. In March 2009, Welch openly turned his back on the concept, calling _____ 'the dumbest idea in the world'.

For a publicly traded company, _____ is the part of its capitalization that is equity as opposed to long-term debt. In the case of only one type of stock, this would roughly be the number of outstanding shares times current shareprice. Things like dividends augment _____ while issuing of shares (stock options) lower it. This _____ added should be compared to average/required increase in value, aka cost of capital.

For a privately held company, the value of the firm after debt must be estimated using one of several valuation methods, s.a. discounted cash flow or others.

Chapter 8. Stock Valuation

a. Cash flow

b. Restricted stock

c. Shareholder value

d. Commercial paper

28. _____ is the planning process used to determine whether a firm's long term investments such as new machinery, replacement machinery, new plants, new products, and research development projects are worth pursuing. It is budget for major capital, or investment, expenditures.

Many formal methods are used in _____, including the techniques such as

- Net present value
- Profitability index
- Internal rate of return
- Modified Internal Rate of Return
- Equivalent annuity

These methods use the incremental cash flows from each potential investment, or project. Techniques based on accounting earnings and accounting rules are sometimes used - though economists consider this to be improper - such as the accounting rate of return, and 'return on investment.' Simplified and hybrid methods are used as well, such as payback period and discounted payback period.

a. Shareholder value

b. Financial distress

c. Preferred stock

d. Capital budgeting

Chapter 9. Capital Budgeting Decision Criteria

1. _____ is the planning process used to determine whether a firm's long term investments such as new machinery, replacement machinery, new plants, new products, and research development projects are worth pursuing. It is budget for major capital, or investment, expenditures.

Many formal methods are used in _____, including the techniques such as

- Net present value
- Profitability index
- Internal rate of return
- Modified Internal Rate of Return
- Equivalent annuity

These methods use the incremental cash flows from each potential investment, or project. Techniques based on accounting earnings and accounting rules are sometimes used - though economists consider this to be improper - such as the accounting rate of return, and 'return on investment.' Simplified and hybrid methods are used as well, such as payback period and discounted payback period.

a. Preferred stock
c. Capital budgeting

b. Shareholder value
d. Financial distress

2. The _____ is a capital budgeting metric used by firms to decide whether they should make investments. It is an indicator of the efficiency or quality of an investment, as opposed to net present value (NPV), which indicates value or magnitude.

The IRR is the annualized effective compounded return rate which can be earned on the invested capital, i.e., the yield on the investment.

a. AAB
c. A Random Walk Down Wall Street

b. ABN Amro
d. Internal rate of return

3. _____ is a financial measure used to determine the attractiveness of an investment. It is generally used as part of a capital budgeting process to rank various alternative choices. It is a modification of the Internal Rate of Return (IRR).

_____ ranks project efficiency consistently with the present worth ratio (variant of NPV/Discounted Negative Cash Flow), considered the gold standard in many finance textbooks.

MIRR is calculated as follows:

width=747 border=0>

where n is the number of (equal) periods in which the cash flows occur.

Chapter 9. Capital Budgeting Decision Criteria

a. Current yield
b. Black-Scholes
c. Binomial options pricing model
d. Modified Internal Rate of Return

4. _____ in business and economics refers to the period of time required for the return on an investment to 'repay' the sum of the original investment. For example, a $1000 investment which returned $500 per year would have a two year _____. It intuitively measures how long something takes to 'pay for itself.' _____ is widely used due to its ease of use despite recognized limitations.

a. Payback period
b. Financial Gerontology
c. Consignment stock
d. Seasoned equity offering

5. In finance, _____, also known as return on investment is the ratio of money gained or lost on an investment relative to the amount of money invested. The amount of money gained or lost may be referred to as interest, profit/loss, gain/loss, or net income/loss. The money invested may be referred to as the asset, capital, principal, or the cost basis of the investment.

a. Stock or scrip dividends
b. Rate of return
c. Composiition of Creditors
d. Doctrine of the Proper Law

6. _____ or net present worth (NPW) is defined as the total present value (PV) of a time series of cash flows. It is a standard method for using the time value of money to appraise long-term projects. Used for capital budgeting, and widely throughout economics, it measures the excess or shortfall of cash flows, in present value terms, once financing charges are met.

a. Negative gearing
b. Net present value
c. Tax shield
d. Present value of costs

7. _____ is the value on a given date of a future payment or series of future payments, discounted to reflect the time value of money and other factors such as investment risk. _____ calculations are widely used in business and economics to provide a means to compare cash flows at different times on a meaningful 'like to like' basis.

The most commonly applied model of the time value of money is compound interest.

a. Present value of benefits
b. Net present value
c. Negative gearing
d. Present value

8. _____ identifies the relationship of investment to payoff of a proposed project. The ratio is calculated as follows:

- >

_____ is also known as Profit Investment Ratio, abbreviated to P.I. and Value Investment Ratio (V.I.R.). _____ is a good tool for ranking projects because it allows you to clearly identify the amount of value created per unit of investment, thus if you are capital constrained you wish to invest in those projects which create value most efficiently first.

a. Conditional prepayment rate
b. Profitability index
c. Capitalization rate
d. Total return

Chapter 9. Capital Budgeting Decision Criteria

9. _____ is the balance of the amounts of cash being received and paid by a business during a defined period of time, sometimes tied to a specific project. Measurement of _____ can be used

- to evaluate the state or performance of a business or project.
- to determine problems with liquidity. Being profitable does not necessarily mean being liquid. A company can fail because of a shortage of cash, even while profitable.
- to generate project rate of returns. The time of _____s into and out of projects are used as inputs to financial models such as internal rate of return, and net present value.
- to examine income or growth of a business when it is believed that accrual accounting concepts do not represent economic realities. Alternately, _____ can be used to 'validate' the net income generated by accrual accounting.

_____ as a generic term may be used differently depending on context, and certain _____ definitions may be adapted by analysts and users for their own uses. Common terms include operating _____ and free _____.

_____s can be classified into:

1. Operational _____s: Cash received or expended as a result of the company's core business activities.
2. Investment _____s: Cash received or expended through capital expenditure, investments or acquisitions.
3. Financing _____s: Cash received or expended as a result of financial activities, such as interests and dividends.

All three together - the net _____ - are necessary to reconcile the beginning cash balance to the ending cash balance. Loan draw downs or equity injections, that is just shifting of capital but no expenditure as such, are not considered in the net _____.

a. Cash flow
b. Shareholder value
c. Corporate finance
d. Real option

10. In finance, the value of an option consists of two components, its intrinsic value and its _____. Time value is simply the difference between option value and intrinsic value. _____ is also known as theta, extrinsic value, or instrumental value.
a. Conservatism
b. Debt buyer
c. Global Squeeze
d. Time value

11. _____ or financing is to provide capital (funds), which means money for a project, a person, a business or any other private or public institutions.

Those funds can be allocated for either short term or long term purposes. The health fund is a new way of _____ private healthcare centers.

a. Synthetic CDO
b. Product life cycle
c. Proxy fight
d. Funding

12. A _____ is an entity formed between two or more parties to undertake economic activity together. The parties agree to create a new entity by both contributing equity, and they then share in the revenues, expenses, and control of the enterprise. The venture can be for one specific project only, or a continuing business relationship such as the Sony Ericsson _____.
    a. Fair Debt Collection Practices Act
    b. Joint venture
    c. Pre-emption right
    d. Lien

Chapter 10. Cash Flows and Other Topics in Capital Budgeting

1. _____ is the task of determining how a business will afford to achieve its strategic goals and objectives. Usually, a company creates a Financial Plan immediately after the vision and objectives have been set. The Financial Plan describes each of the activities, resources, equipment and materials that are needed to achieve these objectives, as well as the timeframes involved.

   a. Performance measurement
   b. Corporate Transparency
   c. Management by exception
   d. Financial planning

2. _____ is the planning process used to determine whether a firm's long term investments such as new machinery, replacement machinery, new plants, new products, and research development projects are worth pursuing. It is budget for major capital, or investment, expenditures.

   Many formal methods are used in _____, including the techniques such as

   - Net present value
   - Profitability index
   - Internal rate of return
   - Modified Internal Rate of Return
   - Equivalent annuity

   These methods use the incremental cash flows from each potential investment, or project. Techniques based on accounting earnings and accounting rules are sometimes used - though economists consider this to be improper - such as the accounting rate of return, and 'return on investment.' Simplified and hybrid methods are used as well, such as payback period and discounted payback period.

   a. Shareholder value
   b. Preferred stock
   c. Financial distress
   d. Capital budgeting

3. _____ is the balance of the amounts of cash being received and paid by a business during a defined period of time, sometimes tied to a specific project. Measurement of _____ can be used

   - to evaluate the state or performance of a business or project.
   - to determine problems with liquidity. Being profitable does not necessarily mean being liquid. A company can fail because of a shortage of cash, even while profitable.
   - to generate project rate of returns. The time of _____s into and out of projects are used as inputs to financial models such as internal rate of return, and net present value.
   - to examine income or growth of a business when it is believed that accrual accounting concepts do not represent economic realities. Alternately, _____ can be used to 'validate' the net income generated by accrual accounting.

   _____ as a generic term may be used differently depending on context, and certain _____ definitions may be adapted by analysts and users for their own uses. Common terms include operating _____ and free _____.

Chapter 10. Cash Flows and Other Topics in Capital Budgeting

_____s can be classified into:

1. Operational _____s: Cash received or expended as a result of the company's core business activities.
2. Investment _____s: Cash received or expended through capital expenditure, investments or acquisitions.
3. Financing _____s: Cash received or expended as a result of financial activities, such as interests and dividends.

All three together - the net _____ - are necessary to reconcile the beginning cash balance to the ending cash balance. Loan draw downs or equity injections, that is just shifting of capital but no expenditure as such, are not considered in the net _____.

a. Cash flow
c. Shareholder value
b. Real option
d. Corporate finance

4. In corporate finance, _____ is a cash flow available for distribution among all the security holders of a company. They include equity holders, debt holders, preferred stock holders, convertible security holders, and so on.

Note that the first three lines above are calculated for you on the standard Statement of Cash Flows.

a. Free cash flow
c. Forfaiting
b. Safety stock
d. Funding

5. The _____ is a capital budgeting metric used by firms to decide whether they should make investments. It is an indicator of the efficiency or quality of an investment, as opposed to net present value (NPV), which indicates value or magnitude.

The IRR is the annualized effective compounded return rate which can be earned on the invested capital, i.e., the yield on the investment.

a. A Random Walk Down Wall Street
c. ABN Amro
b. AAB
d. Internal rate of return

6. _____ is a financial measure used to determine the attractiveness of an investment. It is generally used as part of a capital budgeting process to rank various alternative choices. It is a modification of the Internal Rate of Return (IRR).

_____ ranks project efficiency consistently with the present worth ratio (variant of NPV/Discounted Negative Cash Flow), considered the gold standard in many finance textbooks.

MIRR is calculated as follows:

where n is the number of (equal) periods in which the cash flows occur.

    a. Current yield   b. Black-Scholes
    c. Modified Internal Rate of Return   d. Binomial options pricing model

7. _____ is the provision of resources (such as granting a loan) by one party to another party where that second party does not reimburse the first party immediately, thereby generating a debt, and instead arranges either to repay or return those resources (or material(s) of equal value) at a later date. The first party is called a creditor, also known as a lender, while the second party is called a debtor, also known as a borrower.

Movements of financial capital are normally dependent on either _____ or equity transfers.

    a. Comparable   b. Credit
    c. Warrant   d. Clearing house

8. In finance, _____, also known as return on investment is the ratio of money gained or lost on an investment relative to the amount of money invested. The amount of money gained or lost may be referred to as interest, profit/loss, gain/loss, or net income/loss. The money invested may be referred to as the asset, capital, principal, or the cost basis of the investment.

    a. Doctrine of the Proper Law   b. Composiition of Creditors
    c. Stock or scrip dividends   d. Rate of return

9. In economics, the concept of the _____ refers to the decision-making time frame of a firm in which at least one factor of production is fixed. Costs which are fixed in the _____ have no impact on a firms decisions. For example a firm can raise output by increasing the amount of labour through overtime.

    a. Short-run   b. Long-run
    c. 4-4-5 Calendar   d. 529 plan

10. _____ or economic opportunity loss is the value of the next best alternative foregone as the result of making a decision. _____ analysis is an important part of a company's decision-making processes but is not treated as an actual cost in any financial statement. The next best thing that a person can engage in is referred to as the _____ of doing the best thing and ignoring the next best thing to be done.

    a. AAB   b. ABN Amro
    c. A Random Walk Down Wall Street   d. Opportunity cost

11. In economics and business decision-making, _____ are costs that cannot be recovered once they have been incurred. _____ are sometimes contrasted with variable costs, which are the costs that will change due to the proposed course of action, and prospective costs which are costs that will be incurred if an action is taken. In microeconomic theory, only variable costs are relevant to a decision.

Chapter 10. Cash Flows and Other Topics in Capital Budgeting

a. Hindsight bias
b. Sunk costs
c. 4-4-5 Calendar
d. Hyperbolic discounting

12. In economics, business, and accounting, a _____ is the value of money that has been used up to produce something, and hence is not available for use anymore. In business, the _____ may be one of acquisition, in which case the amount of money expended to acquire it is counted as _____. In this case, money is the input that is gone in order to acquire the thing.
a. Sliding scale fees
b. Marginal cost
c. Fixed costs
d. Cost

13. _____ is a fee paid on borrowed assets. It is the price paid for the use of borrowed money, or, money earned by deposited funds. Assets that are sometimes lent with _____ include money, shares, consumer goods through hire purchase, major assets such as aircraft, and even entire factories in finance lease arrangements.
a. AAB
b. A Random Walk Down Wall Street
c. Insolvency
d. Interest

14. The _____ is the current method of accelerated asset depreciation required by the United States income tax code. Under _____, all assets are divided into classes which dictate the number of years over which an asset's cost will be recovered.

Prior to the Accelerated Cost Recovery System (ACRS), most capital purchases were depreciated using a straight line technique, that allowed for the depreciation of the asset over its useful life.

a. 7-Eleven
b. 529 plan
c. Modified Accelerated Cost Recovery System
d. 4-4-5 Calendar

15. _____ is a term used in accounting, economics and finance to spread the cost of an asset over the span of several years.

In simple words we can say that _____ is the reduction in the value of an asset due to usage, passage of time, wear and tear, technological outdating or obsolescence, depletion or other such factors.

In accounting, _____ is a term used to describe any method of attributing the historical or purchase cost of an asset across its useful life, roughly corresponding to normal wear and tear.

a. Matching principle
b. Deferred financing costs
c. Depreciation
d. Bottom line

16. In business, _____ is income that a company receives from its normal business activities, usually from the sale of goods and services to customers. Some companies also receive _____ from interest, dividends or royalties paid to them by other companies. _____ may refer to business income in general, or it may refer to the amount, in a monetary unit, received during a period of time, as in 'Last year, Company X had _____ of $32 million.'

In many countries, including the UK, _____ is referred to as turnover.

Chapter 10. Cash Flows and Other Topics in Capital Budgeting

a. Bottom line
b. Matching principle
c. Revenue
d. Furniture, Fixtures and Equipment

17. In business and accounting, _____s are everything of value that is owned by a person or company. The balance sheet of a firm records the monetary value of the _____s owned by the firm. The two major _____ classes are tangible _____s and intangible _____s.

a. Income
b. EBITDA
c. Accounts payable
d. Asset

18. In tax accounting the _____ is the default applicable convention used for federal income tax purposes. Like other conventions, the _____ affects the depreciation deduction computation in the year in which the property is placed into service. Using the _____, a taxpayer claims a half of a year's depreciation for the first taxable year, regardless of when the property was actually put into service.

a. 7-Eleven
b. 529 plan
c. 4-4-5 Calendar
d. Half-year convention

19. _____ is a financial metric which represents operating liquidity available to a business. Along with fixed assets such as plant and equipment, _____ is considered a part of operating capital. It is calculated as current assets minus current liabilities.

a. Working capital
b. 529 plan
c. Working capital management
d. 4-4-5 Calendar

20. _____ relates to the cost of borrowing money. It is the price that a lender charges a borrower for the use of the lender's money. _____ is different from OPEX and CAPEX, for it relates to the capital structure of a company.

a. A Random Walk Down Wall Street
b. ABN Amro
c. Interest expense
d. AAB

21. In financial accounting, _____ , cash flow provided by operations or cash flow from operating activities, refers to the amount of cash a company generates from the revenues it brings in, excluding costs associated with long-term investment on capital items or investment in securities.

_____ = Cash generated from operations less taxation and interest paid, investment income received and less dividends paid gives rise to _____s per International Financial Reporting Standards.

To calculate cash generated from operations, one must calculate cash generated from customers and cash paid to suppliers.

a. A Random Walk Down Wall Street
b. Other Comprehensive Basis of Accounting
c. Operating cash flow
d. Appreciation

22. The term _____ is a term applied to practices that are perfunctory, or seek to satisfy the minimum requirements or to conform to a convention or doctrine. It has different meanings in different fields.

In accounting, _____ earnings are those earnings of companies in addition to actual earnings calculated under the Generally Accepted Accounting Principles (GAAP) in their quarterly and yearly financial reports.

a. Pro forma
c. Long-term liabilities
b. Deferred financing costs
d. Deferred income

23. A _____ is the reduction in income taxes that results from taking an allowable deduction from taxable income. For example, because interest on debt is a tax-deductible expense, taking on debt creates a _____. Since a _____ is a way to save cash flows, it increases the value of the business, and it is an important aspect of business valuation.
   a. Refinancing risk
   b. Present value of costs
   c. Present value of benefits
   d. Tax shield

24. An _____ can be defined as a contract which provides an income stream in return for an initial payment.

An immediate _____ is an _____ for which the time between the contract date and the date of the first payment is not longer than the time interval between payments. A common use for an immediate _____ is to provide a pension to a retired person or persons.

   a. AT'T Inc.
   b. Amortization
   c. Annuity
   d. Intrinsic value

25. _____ or financing is to provide capital (funds), which means money for a project, a person, a business or any other private or public institutions.

Those funds can be allocated for either short term or long term purposes. The health fund is a new way of _____ private healthcare centers.

   a. Product life cycle
   b. Synthetic CDO
   c. Funding
   d. Proxy fight

Chapter 11. Capital Budgeting and Risk Analysis

1. _____ is the task of determining how a business will afford to achieve its strategic goals and objectives. Usually, a company creates a Financial Plan immediately after the vision and objectives have been set. The Financial Plan describes each of the activities, resources, equipment and materials that are needed to achieve these objectives, as well as the timeframes involved.

   a. Corporate Transparency
   b. Financial planning
   c. Management by exception
   d. Performance measurement

2. The _____ is a capital budgeting metric used by firms to decide whether they should make investments. It is an indicator of the efficiency or quality of an investment, as opposed to net present value (NPV), which indicates value or magnitude.

   The IRR is the annualized effective compounded return rate which can be earned on the invested capital, i.e., the yield on the investment.

   a. AAB
   b. ABN Amro
   c. A Random Walk Down Wall Street
   d. Internal rate of return

3. _____ is a financial measure used to determine the attractiveness of an investment. It is generally used as part of a capital budgeting process to rank various alternative choices. It is a modification of the Internal Rate of Return (IRR).

   _____ ranks project efficiency consistently with the present worth ratio (variant of NPV/Discounted Negative Cash Flow), considered the gold standard in many finance textbooks.

   MIRR is calculated as follows:

   width=747 border=0>

   where n is the number of (equal) periods in which the cash flows occur.

   a. Modified Internal Rate of Return
   b. Current yield
   c. Binomial options pricing model
   d. Black-Scholes

4. In finance, _____ is that risk which is common to an entire market and not to any individual entity or component thereof. It should be distinguished from systemic risk which is the risk that the entire financial system will collapse as a result of some catastrophic event.

   Risks can be reduced in four main ways: Avoidance, Reduction, Retention and Transfer.

   a. Conglomerate merger
   b. Capital surplus
   c. Primary market
   d. Systematic risk

5. In finance, _____, also known as return on investment is the ratio of money gained or lost on an investment relative to the amount of money invested. The amount of money gained or lost may be referred to as interest, profit/loss, gain/loss, or net income/loss. The money invested may be referred to as the asset, capital, principal, or the cost basis of the investment.

Chapter 11. Capital Budgeting and Risk Analysis

a. Stock or scrip dividends
c. Composiition of Creditors
b. Doctrine of the Proper Law
d. Rate of return

6. _____ is the planning process used to determine whether a firm's long term investments such as new machinery, replacement machinery, new plants, new products, and research development projects are worth pursuing. It is budget for major capital, or investment, expenditures.

Many formal methods are used in _____, including the techniques such as

- Net present value
- Profitability index
- Internal rate of return
- Modified Internal Rate of Return
- Equivalent annuity

These methods use the incremental cash flows from each potential investment, or project. Techniques based on accounting earnings and accounting rules are sometimes used - though economists consider this to be improper - such as the accounting rate of return, and 'return on investment.' Simplified and hybrid methods are used as well, such as payback period and discounted payback period.

a. Shareholder value
c. Preferred stock
b. Financial distress
d. Capital budgeting

7. The _____ is the guaranteed payoff at which a person is 'indifferent' between accepting the guaranteed payoff and a higher but uncertain payoff. (It is the amount of the higher payout minus the risk premium).

a. Certainty equivalent
c. 4-4-5 Calendar
b. 7-Eleven
d. 529 plan

8. A '_____' is a 'Charge' that is paid to obtain the right to delay a payment. Essentially, the payer purchases the right to make a given payment in the future instead of in the Present. The '_____', or 'Charge' that must be paid to delay the payment, is simply the difference between what the payment amount would be if it were paid in the present and what the payment amount would be paid if it were paid in the future.

a. Discount
c. Risk aversion
b. Value at risk
d. Risk modeling

9. The _____ is an interest rate a central bank charges depository institutions that borrow reserves from it.

Chapter 11. Capital Budgeting and Risk Analysis

The term _____ has two meanings:

- the same as interest rate; the term 'discount' does not refer to the meaning of the word, but to the purpose of using the quantity, such as computations of present value, e.g. net present value / discounted cash flow

- the annual effective _____, which is the annual interest divided by the capital including that interest; this rate is lower than the interest rate; it corresponds to using the value after a year as the nominal value, and seeing the initial value as the nominal value minus a discount; it is used for Treasury Bills and similar financial instruments

The annual effective _____ is the annual interest divided by the capital including that interest, which is the interest rate divided by 100% plus the interest rate. It is the annual discount factor to be applied to the future cash flow, to find the discount, subtracted from a future value to find the value one year earlier.

For example, suppose there is a government bond that sells for $95 and pays $100 in a year's time.

a. Stochastic volatility
c. Black-Scholes
b. Discount rate
d. Fisher equation

10. In e-business terms, a _____ is an organization that originated and does business purely through the internet, they have no physical store (brick and mortar) where customers can shop. Examples of large _____ companies include Amazon.com and Netflix.com. There are also many smaller, niche oriented _____ mail order companies such as women's travel accessories company Christine Columbus and fashion jewelry merchant Jewels of Denial.

a. Pure play
c. The Dogs of the Dow
b. 529 plan
d. 4-4-5 Calendar

11. _____ is a process of analyzing possible future events by considering alternative possible outcomes (scenarios.) The analysis is designed to allow improved decision-making by allowing consideration of outcomes and their implications.

For example, in economics and finance, a financial institution might attempt to forecast several possible scenarios for the economy (e.g. rapid growth, moderate growth, slow growth) and it might also attempt to forecast financial market returns (for bonds, stocks and cash) in each of those scenarios.

a. 529 plan
c. Detection Risk
b. 4-4-5 Calendar
d. Scenario analysis

12. _____ is the study of how the variation (uncertainty) in the output of a mathematical model can be apportioned, qualitatively or quantitatively, to different sources of variation in the input of a model.

In more general terms uncertainty and sensitivity analyses investigate the robustness of a study when the study includes some form of mathematical modelling. While uncertainty analysis studies the overall uncertainty in the conclusions of the study, _____ tries to identify what source of uncertainty weights more on the study's conclusions.

Chapter 11. Capital Budgeting and Risk Analysis

a. Synthetic CDO
b. Golden parachute
c. Proxy fight
d. Sensitivity analysis

13. _____ is the balance of the amounts of cash being received and paid by a business during a defined period of time, sometimes tied to a specific project. Measurement of _____ can be used

- to evaluate the state or performance of a business or project.
- to determine problems with liquidity. Being profitable does not necessarily mean being liquid. A company can fail because of a shortage of cash, even while profitable.
- to generate project rate of returns. The time of _____s into and out of projects are used as inputs to financial models such as internal rate of return, and net present value.
- to examine income or growth of a business when it is believed that accrual accounting concepts do not represent economic realities. Alternately, _____ can be used to 'validate' the net income generated by accrual accounting.

_____ as a generic term may be used differently depending on context, and certain _____ definitions may be adapted by analysts and users for their own uses. Common terms include operating _____ and free _____.

_____s can be classified into:

1. Operational _____s: Cash received or expended as a result of the company's core business activities.
2. Investment _____s: Cash received or expended through capital expenditure, investments or acquisitions.
3. Financing _____s: Cash received or expended as a result of financial activities, such as interests and dividends.

All three together - the net _____ - are necessary to reconcile the beginning cash balance to the ending cash balance. Loan draw downs or equity injections, that is just shifting of capital but no expenditure as such, are not considered in the net _____.

a. Shareholder value
b. Real option
c. Cash Flow
d. Corporate finance

14. _____ is the probability of some event A, given the occurrence of some other event B. _____ is written P(A│B), and is read 'the probability of A, given B'.

Joint probability is the probability of two events in conjunction. That is, it is the probability of both events together.

a. 7-Eleven
b. 529 plan
c. Conditional probability
d. 4-4-5 Calendar

15. _____ or financing is to provide capital (funds), which means money for a project, a person, a business or any other private or public institutions.

Those funds can be allocated for either short term or long term purposes. The health fund is a new way of _____ private healthcare centers.

a. Synthetic CDO
b. Product life cycle
c. Proxy fight
d. Funding

16. In economics, business, and accounting, a _____ is the value of money that has been used up to produce something, and hence is not available for use anymore. In business, the _____ may be one of acquisition, in which case the amount of money expended to acquire it is counted as _____. In this case, money is the input that is gone in order to acquire the thing.

a. Sliding scale fees
b. Fixed costs
c. Marginal cost
d. Cost

17. The _____ is an expected return that the provider of capital plans to earn on their investment.

Capital (money) used for funding a business should earn returns for the capital providers who risk their capital. For an investment to be worthwhile, the expected return on capital must be greater than the _____.

a. Cost of capital
b. 4-4-5 Calendar
c. Capital intensity
d. Weighted average cost of capital

Chapter 12. Cost of Capital

1. Briggs could refer to:

   - Briggs cliff, a fictional place in Fullmetal Alchemist manga
   - Briggs (crater), a lunar crater
   - Briggs Initiative, either of two pieces of Californian legislation sponsored by John Briggs
   - Briggs Islet, Tasmania, Australia
   - Briggs, Oklahoma, USA
   - Briggs, Texas, USA
   - _____, a manufacturer of air-cooled gasoline engines
   - The Briggs - a punk rock band
   - Myers-Briggs Type Indicator

   - Anne Briggs, English folk singer
   - Ansel Briggs, American politician
   - Arthur E. Briggs, California politician
   - Asa Briggs, British historian
   - Barbara Briggs, American dramatist
   - Barbara G. Briggs, Australian botanist
   - Barry Briggs, New Zealand World Motorcycle speedway champion
   - Barry Bruce-Briggs, public policy writer
   - Benjamin Briggs, captain of the Mary Celeste
   - Bill Briggs, American skier
   - Billy Briggs, American musician
   - Bobby Briggs, fictional character from Twin Peaks
   - Charles Augustus Briggs, American theologian
   - Charles Frederick Briggs, American journalist
   - Clare Briggs, American comics artist
   - David Briggs:
     - David Briggs (producer) (1944-1995), American record producer
     - David Briggs (composer) English organist and composer
     - David Briggs (Australian musician) , guitarist with Little River Band and Australian record producer
   - Derek Briggs, Irish paleontologist
   - Everett Francis Briggs, (1908-2006), American Catholic priest
   - Frank A. Briggs, American politician
   - Frank O. Briggs, American politician
   - Frank P. Briggs, American politician
   - Gary Briggs (musician), British guitarist
   - Gary Briggs (footballer), British footballer
   - George N. Briggs, American politician
   - Major Garland Briggs, fictional character from Twin Peaks
   - Harold Briggs
     - Harold Briggs (General), British general
     - Harold Briggs (politician), British Conservative MP
   - Henry Briggs (politician)
   - Henry Briggs (mathematician), English mathematician
   - Hortense Briggs, fictional character from An American Tragedy by Theodore Dreiser
   - Ian Briggs, television writer
   - Jack Briggs, American instrument maker
   - James Briggs, any of several people
   - Jason W. Briggs, American Latter Day Saint leader
   - Jeff Briggs, American composer and former computer games executive
   - Joe Bob Briggs, pseudonym of John Irving Bloom, film critic and actor
   - John Briggs (politician), a California politician
   - John Briggs (author)
   - Johnny Briggs:

- - Johnny Briggs (cricketer)
  - Johnny Briggs (actor), actor who played Mike Baldwin on the British soap opera Coronation Street
  - Johnny Briggs (baseball), a former Major League Baseball outfielder
- Jon Briggs, British radio personality
- Jonny Briggs, BBC children's television programme first broadcast in 1985.
- Karen Briggs, American violinist
- Katharine Cook Briggs, co-inventor of the Myers-Briggs Type Indicator personality test
- Katharine Mary Briggs, British author
- Kevin 'She'kspere' Briggs, American record producer
- Lance Briggs, American football player
- LeBaron Russell Briggs, American educator
- Luke Briggs, British Steward
- Lyman James Briggs, American physicist and civil servant
- Matilda Briggs, passenger on the Marie Celeste
- Matthew Briggs, English footballer
- Nicholas Briggs, British actor
- Nigel Briggs, Singer/Song writer
- Patricia Briggs, American fantasy writer
- Paul Briggs, Australian boxer
- Raymond Briggs, British illustrator and author
- Sandra Briggs, fictional character from Emmerdale
- Shannon Briggs, American boxer
- Stephen Briggs, British Discworld adapter
- Stephen Foster Briggs, American engineer, co-founder of The _____ Company
- Ted Briggs, British seaman
- Tom Briggs, American football player
- Walter Briggs, Major League Baseball owner

Chapter 12. Cost of Capital

a. 4-4-5 Calendar
b. 529 plan
c. 7-Eleven
d. Briggs ' Stratton

2. _____, is when a company issues common stock or shares to the public for the first time. They are often issued by smaller, younger companies seeking capital to expand, but can also be done by large privately-owned companies looking to become publicly traded.

In an _____ the issuer may obtain the assistance of an underwriting firm, which helps it determine what type of security to issue (common or preferred), best offering price and time to bring it to market.

a. Initial public offering
b. Asian Financial Crisis
c. Insolvency
d. Interest

3. The _____ is the rate that a company is expected to pay to finance its assets. WACC is the minimum return that a company must earn on existing asset base to satisfy its creditors, owners, and other providers of capital.

Companies raise money from a number of sources: common equity, preferred equity, straight debt, convertible debt, exchangeable debt, warrants, options, pension liabilities, executive stock options, governmental subsidies, and so on.

a. 4-4-5 Calendar
b. Weighted average cost of capital
c. Cost of capital
d. Capital intensity

4. In economics, business, and accounting, a _____ is the value of money that has been used up to produce something, and hence is not available for use anymore. In business, the _____ may be one of acquisition, in which case the amount of money expended to acquire it is counted as _____. In this case, money is the input that is gone in order to acquire the thing.

a. Fixed costs
b. Marginal cost
c. Sliding scale fees
d. Cost

5. The _____ is an expected return that the provider of capital plans to earn on their investment.

Capital (money) used for funding a business should earn returns for the capital providers who risk their capital. For an investment to be worthwhile, the expected return on capital must be greater than the _____.

a. Cost of capital
b. Capital intensity
c. Weighted average cost of capital
d. 4-4-5 Calendar

6. In finance, _____, also known as return on investment is the ratio of money gained or lost on an investment relative to the amount of money invested. The amount of money gained or lost may be referred to as interest, profit/loss, gain/loss, or net income/loss. The money invested may be referred to as the asset, capital, principal, or the cost basis of the investment.

a. Composiition of Creditors
b. Rate of return
c. Stock or scrip dividends
d. Doctrine of the Proper Law

7. In finance, the _____ is used to determine a theoretically appropriate required rate of return of an asset, if that asset is to be added to an already well-diversified portfolio, given that asset's non-diversifiable risk. The model takes into account the asset's sensitivity to non-diversifiable risk (also known as systemic risk or market risk), often represented by the quantity beta (β) in the financial industry, as well as the expected return of the market and the expected return of a theoretical risk-free asset.

The model was introduced by Jack Treynor (1961, 1962), William Sharpe (1964), John Lintner (1965a,b) and Jan Mossin (1966) independently, building on the earlier work of Harry Markowitz on diversification and modern portfolio theory.

   a. Random walk hypothesis   b. Hull-White model
   c. Cox-Ingersoll-Ross model   d. Capital asset pricing model

8. _____ is that which is owed; usually referencing assets owed, but the term can cover other obligations. In the case of assets, _____ is a means of using future purchasing power in the present before a summation has been earned. Some companies and corporations use _____ as a part of their overall corporate finance strategy.
   a. Credit cycle   b. Partial Payment
   c. Debt   d. Cross-collateralization

9. _____ is a form of corporation equity ownership represented in the securities. It is dangerous in comparison to preferred shares and some other investment options, in that in the event of bankruptcy, _____ investors receive their funds after preferred stockholders, bondholders, creditors, etc. On the other hand, common shares on average perform better than preferred shares or bonds over time.
   a. Common stock   b. Stock market bubble
   c. Stock split   d. Stop-limit order

10. _____ is typically a higher ranking stock than voting shares, and its terms are negotiated between the corporation and the investor.

_____ usually carry no voting rights, but may carry superior priority over common stock in the payment of dividends and upon liquidation. _____ may carry a dividend that is paid out prior to any dividends to common stock holders.

   a. Trade-off theory   b. Second lien loan
   c. Follow-on offering   d. Preferred stock

11. In business and accounting, _____s are everything of value that is owned by a person or company. The balance sheet of a firm records the monetary value of the _____s owned by the firm. The two major _____ classes are tangible _____s and intangible _____s.
   a. EBITDA   b. Accounts payable
   c. Income   d. Asset

12. A _____ is a payment made by a corporation to its shareholder members. When a corporation earns a profit or surplus, that money can be put to two uses: it can either be re-invested in the business (called retained earnings), or it can be paid to the shareholders as a _____. Many corporations retain a portion of their earnings and pay the remainder as a _____.

Chapter 12. Cost of Capital

a. Dividend yield
c. Dividend puzzle
b. Special dividend
d. Dividend

13. The term _____ has three unrelated technical definitions, and is also used in a variety of non-technical ways.

- In financial economics, it refers to any asset used to make money, as opposed to assets used for personal enjoyment or consumption. This is an important distinction because two people can disagree sharply about the value of personal assets, one person might think a sports car is more valuable than a pickup truck, another person might have the opposite taste. But if an asset is held for the purpose of making money, taste has nothing to do with it, only differences of opinion about how much money the asset will produce. With the further assumption that people agree on the probability distribution of future cash flows, it is possible to have an objective _____ pricing model. Even without the assumption of agreement, it is possible to set rational limits on _____ value.
- In governmental accounting, it is defined as any asset used in operations with an initial useful life extending beyond one reporting period. Generally, government managers have a 'stewardship' duty to maintain _____s under their control. See International Public Sector Accounting Standards for details.
- In US tax accounting, it is defined as any property other than a list of exceptions. The main exceptions are anything held for sale, and any real estate or depreciable property used in business. Almost everything you own and use for personal purposes, pleasure or investment is a _____. If something is a _____ for tax purposes, gains or losses on sale or disposition are capital gains or capital losses. For individuals, however, capital losses on property held for personal use are generally not deductible. See the IRS publication Tax Facts about Capital Gains and Losses for details.

A well-known financial accounting textbook advises that the term be avoided except in tax accounting because it is used in so many different senses, not all of them well-defined. For example it is often used as a synonym for fixed assets or for investments in securities.

A common non-technical usage occurs when people ask that employees or the environment or something else be treated as a _____.

a. Settlement date
c. Solvency
b. Political risk
d. Capital asset

14. In finance, _____ is the process of estimating the potential market value of a financial asset or liability. they can be done on assets (for example, investments in marketable securities such as stocks, options, business enterprises, or intangible assets such as patents and trademarks) or on liabilities (e.g., Bonds issued by a company.) _____s are required in many contexts including investment analysis, capital budgeting, merger and acquisition transactions, financial reporting, taxable events to determine the proper tax liability, and in litigation.

a. Procter ' Gamble
c. Share
b. Margin
d. Valuation

15. In business and finance, a _____ (also referred to as equity _____) of stock means a _____ of ownership in a corporation (company.) In the plural, stocks is often used as a synonym for _____s especially in the United States, but it is less commonly used that way outside of North America.

In the United Kingdom, South Africa, and Australia, stock can also refer to completely different financial instruments such as government bonds or, less commonly, to all kinds of marketable securities.

a. Procter ' Gamble
c. Bucket shop
b. Margin
d. Share

16. In finance, _____ refers to the way a corporation finances its assets through some combination of equity, debt, or hybrid securities. A firm's _____ is then the composition or 'structure' of its liabilities. For example, a firm that sells $20 billion in equity and $80 billion in debt is said to be 20% equity-financed and 80% debt-financed.
   a. Market for corporate control
   c. Capital structure
   b. Rights issue
   d. Book building

17. The U.S. _____ is an independent agency of the United States government which holds primary responsibility for enforcing the federal securities laws and regulating the securities industry, the nation's stock and options exchanges, and other electronic securities markets. The SEC was created by section 4 of the SEC of 1934 (now codified as 15 U.S.C. § 78d and commonly referred to as the 1934 Act.)
   a. 7-Eleven
   c. 529 plan
   b. Securities and Exchange Commission
   d. 4-4-5 Calendar

18. _____ is the planning process used to determine whether a firm's long term investments such as new machinery, replacement machinery, new plants, new products, and research development projects are worth pursuing. It is budget for major capital, or investment, expenditures.

Many formal methods are used in _____, including the techniques such as

- Net present value
- Profitability index
- Internal rate of return
- Modified Internal Rate of Return
- Equivalent annuity

These methods use the incremental cash flows from each potential investment, or project. Techniques based on accounting earnings and accounting rules are sometimes used - though economists consider this to be improper - such as the accounting rate of return, and 'return on investment.' Simplified and hybrid methods are used as well, such as payback period and discounted payback period.

   a. Financial distress
   c. Preferred stock
   b. Shareholder value
   d. Capital budgeting

19. _____ is normally any risk associated with any form of financing.

Depending on the nature of the investment, the type of 'investment' risk will vary. High risk investments have greater potential rewards, but you may lose your money instead by taking the risk for more money.

   a. Liquidating dividend
   c. Revaluation
   b. Stock market index option
   d. Financial risk

20. In economics, the _____ is the proposition by Irving Fisher that the real interest rate is independent of monetary measures, especially the nominal interest rate. The Fisher equation is

Chapter 12. Cost of Capital

$r_r = r_n >- >\pi^e$.

This means, the real interest rate (r_r) equals the nominal interest rate (r_n) minus expected rate of inflation ($>\pi^e$.) Here all the rates are continuously compounded.

a. 7-Eleven
b. 529 plan
c. Fisher hypothesis
d. 4-4-5 Calendar

21. _____ is a fee paid on borrowed assets. It is the price paid for the use of borrowed money, or, money earned by deposited funds. Assets that are sometimes lent with _____ include money, shares, consumer goods through hire purchase, major assets such as aircraft, and even entire factories in finance lease arrangements.
a. AAB
b. Interest
c. Insolvency
d. A Random Walk Down Wall Street

22. An _____ is the price a borrower pays for the use of money they do not own, and the return a lender receives for deferring the use of funds, by lending it to the borrower. _____s are normally expressed as a percentage rate over the period of one year.

_____s targets are also a vital tool of monetary policy and are used to control variables like investment, inflation, and unemployment.

a. AAB
b. ABN Amro
c. A Random Walk Down Wall Street
d. Interest rate

23. _____ is an economic concept, expressed as a basic algebraic identity that relates interest rates and exchange rates. The identity is theoretical, and usually follows from assumptions imposed in economics models. There is evidence to support as well as to refute the concept.
a. A Random Walk Down Wall Street
b. AAB
c. Unit price
d. Interest rate parity

24. The _____ is a hypothesis in international finance that says that the difference in the nominal interest rates between two countries determines the movement of the nominal exchange rate between their currencies, with the value of the currency of the country with the lower nominal interest rate increasing. This is also known as the assumption of Uncovered Interest Parity.

The Fisher hypothesis says that the real interest rate in an economy is independent of monetary variables.

a. A Random Walk Down Wall Street
b. International Fisher effect
c. Interest rate risk
d. Official bank rate

25. In finance, a _____ is a debt security, in which the authorized issuer owes the holders a debt and, depending on the terms of the _____, is obliged to pay interest (the coupon) and/or to repay the principal at a later date, termed maturity.

Thus a _____ is a loan: the issuer is the borrower, the _____ holder is the lender, and the coupon is the interest. _____s provide the borrower with external funds to finance long-term investments, or, in the case of government _____s, to finance current expenditure.

a. Puttable bond
c. Convertible bond
b. Catastrophe bonds
d. Bond

26. In finance, the _____ between two currencies specifies how much one currency is worth in terms of the other. For example an _____ of 102 Japanese yen to the United States dollar means that JPY 102 is worth the same as USD 1. The foreign exchange market is one of the largest markets in the world.

a. A Random Walk Down Wall Street
c. AAB
b. ABN Amro
d. Exchange rate

27. In financial accounting, the term _____ is most commonly used to describe any part of shareholders' equity, except for basic share capital. Sometimes, the term is used instead of the term provision; such a use, however, is inconsistent with the terminology suggested by International Accounting Standards Board. For more information about provisions, see provision (accounting.)

a. FIFO and LIFO accounting
c. Treasury stock
b. Closing entries
d. Reserve

28. A _____, reserve bank, or monetary authority is the entity responsible for the monetary policy of a country or of a group of member states. It is a bank that can lend money to other banks in times of need. Its primary responsibility is to maintain the stability of the national currency and money supply, but more active duties include controlling subsidized-loan interest rates, and acting as a lender of last resort to the banking sector during times of financial crisis (private banks often being integral to the national financial system.)

a. 529 plan
c. 7-Eleven
b. 4-4-5 Calendar
d. Central bank

29. In finance, the yield curve is the relation between the interest rate (or cost of borrowing) and the time to maturity of the debt for a given borrower in a given currency. For example, the current U.S. dollar interest rates paid on U.S. Treasury securities for various maturities are closely watched by many traders, and are commonly plotted on a graph such as the one on the right which is informally called 'the yield curve.' More formal mathematical descriptions of this relation are often called the _____.

The yield of a debt instrument is the annualized percentage increase in the value of the investment.

a. 529 plan
c. 4-4-5 Calendar
b. 7-Eleven
d. Term structure of interest rates

30. _____ is a business buzz term, which implies that the ultimate measure of a company's success is to enrich shareholders. It became popular during the 1980s, and is particularly associated with former CEO of General Electric, Jack Welch. In March 2009, Welch openly turned his back on the concept, calling _____ 'the dumbest idea in the world'.

Chapter 12. Cost of Capital

For a publicly traded company, _____ is the part of its capitalization that is equity as opposed to long-term debt. In the case of only one type of stock, this would roughly be the number of outstanding shares times current shareprice. Things like dividends augment _____ while issuing of shares (stock options) lower it. This _____ added should be compared to average/required increase in value, aka cost of capital.

For a privately held company, the value of the firm after debt must be estimated using one of several valuation methods, s.a. discounted cash flow or others.

a. Cash flow
b. Shareholder value
c. Restricted stock
d. Commercial paper

Chapter 13. Managing for Shareholder Value

1. _____ represents the total cash investment that shareholders and debtholders have made in a company. There are two different but completely equivalent methods for calculating _____. The operating approach is calculated as:

_____ = Operating Net Working Capital + Net PP'E + Capitalized Operating Leases + Other Operating Assets + Operating Intangibles - Other Operating Liabilities - Cumulative Adjustment for Amortization of R'D

Equivalently, the financing approach is calculated as:

In symbols:

$$K = D + E - M$$

_____ is used in several important measurements of financial performance, including return on _____, economic value added, and free cash flow.

a. Information ratio
b. Inventory turnover
c. Operating leverage
d. Invested capital

2. _____ is the price at which an asset would trade in a competitive Walrasian auction setting. _____ is often used interchangeably with open _____, fair value or fair _____, although these terms have distinct definitions in different standards, and may differ in some circumstances.

International Valuation Standards defines _____ as 'the estimated amount for which a property should exchange on the date of valuation between a willing buyer and a willing seller in an arm'e;s-length transaction after proper marketing wherein the parties had each acted knowledgeably, prudently, and without compulsion.'

_____ is a concept distinct from market price, which is 'e;the price at which one can transact'e;, while _____ is 'e;the true underlying value'e; according to theoretical standards.

a. Wrap account
b. Debt restructuring
c. T-Model
d. Market value

3. _____ is the difference between the current market value of a firm and the capital contributed by investors. If _____ is positive, the firm has added value. If it is negative, the firm has destroyed value.

a. Decision process tool
b. Monetary system
c. Wrap account
d. Market value added

4. _____ refers to the additional value of a commodity over the cost of commodities used to produce it from the previous stage of production. An example is the price of gasoline at the pump over the price of the oil in it. In national accounts used in macroeconomics, it refers to the contribution of the factors of production, i.e., land, labor, and capital goods, to raising the value of a product and corresponds to the incomes received by the owners of these factors.

a. Demand shock
b. Supply shock
c. Deregulation
d. Value added

Chapter 13. Managing for Shareholder Value

5. _____ is a process and a set of procedures used to estimate the economic value of an owner's interest in a business. Valuation is used by financial market participants to determine the price they are willing to pay or receive to consummate a sale of a business. In addition to estimating the selling price of a business, the same valuation tools are often used by business appraisers to resolve disputes related to estate and gift taxation, divorce litigation, allocate business purchase price among business assets, establish a formula for estimating the value of partners' ownership interest for buy-sell agreements, and many other business and legal purposes.

   a. Covenant
   b. Federal Deposit Insurance Corporation Improvement Act
   c. Family and Medical Leave Act
   d. Business valuation

6. In finance, _____ is the process of estimating the potential market value of a financial asset or liability. they can be done on assets (for example, investments in marketable securities such as stocks, options, business enterprises, or intangible assets such as patents and trademarks) or on liabilities (e.g., Bonds issued by a company.) _____s are required in many contexts including investment analysis, capital budgeting, merger and acquisition transactions, financial reporting, taxable events to determine the proper tax liability, and in litigation.

   a. Margin
   b. Valuation
   c. Share
   d. Procter ' Gamble

7. _____ is a business buzz term, which implies that the ultimate measure of a company's success is to enrich shareholders. It became popular during the 1980s, and is particularly associated with former CEO of General Electric, Jack Welch. In March 2009, Welch openly turned his back on the concept, calling _____ 'the dumbest idea in the world'.

   For a publicly traded company, _____ is the part of its capitalization that is equity as opposed to long-term debt. In the case of only one type of stock, this would roughly be the number of outstanding shares times current shareprice. Things like dividends augment _____ while issuing of shares (stock options) lower it. This _____ added should be compared to average/required increase in value, aka cost of capital.

   For a privately held company, the value of the firm after debt must be estimated using one of several valuation methods, s.a. discounted cash flow or others.

   a. Restricted stock
   b. Commercial paper
   c. Cash flow
   d. Shareholder value

8. _____ is the task of determining how a business will afford to achieve its strategic goals and objectives. Usually, a company creates a Financial Plan immediately after the vision and objectives have been set. The Financial Plan describes each of the activities, resources, equipment and materials that are needed to achieve these objectives, as well as the timeframes involved.

   a. Corporate Transparency
   b. Management by exception
   c. Performance measurement
   d. Financial planning

9. In corporate finance, _____ is a cash flow available for distribution among all the security holders of a company. They include equity holders, debt holders, preferred stock holders, convertible security holders, and so on.

Note that the first three lines above are calculated for you on the standard Statement of Cash Flows.

88   Chapter 13. Managing for Shareholder Value

   a. Forfaiting
   c. Safety stock
   b. Funding
   d. Free cash flow

10. In finance, the _____ (continuing value or horizon value) of a security is the present value at a future point in time of all future cash flows when we expect stable growth rate forever. It is most often used in multi-stage discounted cash flow analysis, and allows for the limitation of cash flow projections to a several-year period. Forecasting results beyond such a period is impractical and exposes such projections to a variety of risks limiting their validity, primarily the great uncertainty involved in predicting industry and macroeconomic conditions beyond a few years.

   a. Negative gearing
   c. Discounted cash flow
   b. Terminal value
   d. Refinancing risk

11. _____ is the balance of the amounts of cash being received and paid by a business during a defined period of time, sometimes tied to a specific project. Measurement of _____ can be used

- to evaluate the state or performance of a business or project.
- to determine problems with liquidity. Being profitable does not necessarily mean being liquid. A company can fail because of a shortage of cash, even while profitable.
- to generate project rate of returns. The time of _____s into and out of projects are used as inputs to financial models such as internal rate of return, and net present value.
- to examine income or growth of a business when it is believed that accrual accounting concepts do not represent economic realities. Alternately, _____ can be used to 'validate' the net income generated by accrual accounting.

_____ as a generic term may be used differently depending on context, and certain _____ definitions may be adapted by analysts and users for their own uses. Common terms include operating _____ and free _____.

_____s can be classified into:

1. Operational _____s: Cash received or expended as a result of the company's core business activities.
2. Investment _____s: Cash received or expended through capital expenditure, investments or acquisitions.
3. Financing _____s: Cash received or expended as a result of financial activities, such as interests and dividends.

All three together - the net _____ - are necessary to reconcile the beginning cash balance to the ending cash balance. Loan draw downs or equity injections, that is just shifting of capital but no expenditure as such, are not considered in the net _____.

   a. Real option
   c. Shareholder value
   b. Corporate finance
   d. Cash flow

12. In corporate finance, _____ is an estimate of true economic profit after making corrective adjustments to GAAP accounting, including deducting the opportunity cost of equity capital. GAAP is estimated to ignore US$300 billion in shareholder opportunity costs. _____ can be measured as Net Operating Profit After Taxes(or NOPAT) less the money cost of capital.

Chapter 13. Managing for Shareholder Value

a. ABN Amro
c. AAB

b. A Random Walk Down Wall Street
d. Economic value added

13. In corporate finance, _____ is a company's after-tax operating profit for all investors, including shareholders and debt holders. It is defined as follows:

_____ = Operating profit x (1 - Tax Rate)

An alternative formula is as follows

_____ = Net Profit After Tax + after tax Interest Expense - after tax Interest Income

For companies with no debt and thus no interest expense, _____ is equal to net profit. In other words, _____ represents the company's operating profit that would accrue to shareholders (after taxes) if the company had no debt.

a. Revaluation
c. Channel stuffing

b. Sector rotation
d. Net operating profit after tax

14. _____ is a measure of a company's earning power from ongoing operations, equal to earnings before the deduction of interest payments and income taxes.

To accountants, economic profit, or EP, is a single-period metric to determine the value created by a company in one period - usually a year. It is the net profit after tax less the equity charge, a risk-weighted cost of capital.

a. AAB
c. Operating profit

b. A Random Walk Down Wall Street
d. Economic profit

15. _____ is the difference between price and the costs of bringing to market whatever it is that is accounted as an enterprise (whether by harvest, extraction, manufacture, or purchase) in terms of the component costs of delivered goods and/or services and any operating or other expenses.

A key difficulty in measuring profit is in defining costs. Pure economic monetary profits can be zero or negative even in competitive equilibrium when accounted monetized costs exceed monetized price.

a. AAB
c. Economic profit

b. Accounting profit
d. A Random Walk Down Wall Street

16. _____ is a financial measure that quantifies how well a company generates cash flow relative to the capital it has invested in its business. It is defined as Net operating profit less adjusted taxes divided by Invested Capital and is usually expressed as a percentage. In this calculation, capital invested includes all monetary capital invested: long-term debt, common and preferred shares.

a. Cash conversion cycle
c. Debt service coverage ratio

b. Sharpe ratio
d. Return on invested capital

Chapter 13. Managing for Shareholder Value

17. In statistics, _____ has two related meanings:

- the arithmetic _____
- the expected value of a random variable, which is also called the population _____.

It is sometimes stated that the '_____' is average. This is incorrect if '_____' is taken in the specific sense of 'arithmetic _____' as there are different types of averages: the _____, median, and mode. Other simple statistical analyses use measures of spread, such as range, interquartile range, or standard deviation. For a real-valued random variable X, the _____ is the expectation of X. Note that not every probability distribution has a defined _____; see the Cauchy distribution for an example.

a. Mean
b. Sample size
c. Probability distribution
d. Harmonic mean

18. In economic models, the _____ time frame assumes no fixed factors of production. Firms can enter or leave the marketplace, and the cost (and availability) of land, labor, raw materials, and capital goods can be assumed to vary. In contrast, in the short-run time frame, certain factors are assumed to be fixed, because there is not sufficient time for them to change.

a. Short-run
b. Long-run
c. 529 plan
d. 4-4-5 Calendar

19. A _____ is heuristic and has the following assumptions :

- Rationality of all market actors (Rationality in meaning of the actor's utility maximization)
- No transaction costs (particularly no information costs and no taxes)
- Price taking behavior - there is a sufficiently large number of participants such that no individual can affect the market
- given rare resources
- freedom of decision to do something or to let it be (no external effects)

Share and foreign exchange markets are commonly seen to be the most similar to the _____. The real estate market is an example of a very imperfect market. a free market economy is also related to this _____ system as the public have free will

Other characteristics of a _____ include:-

- No barriers to entry to (or exit from) the market
- Perfect knowledge
- Normal profits

Normal profits are defined as that level of profit which just induces the participants to stay in the market. In other words companies in a _____ pay no dividends, as super-normal profits would induce other participants into the market and drive profits back to the 'normal' level.

This attribute of _____s has profound political and economic implications, as many people assume that the purpose of the market is to enable participants to make profits.

Chapter 13. Managing for Shareholder Value

a. 4-4-5 Calendar
c. 529 plan
b. 7-Eleven
d. Perfect market

20. In economics, the concept of the _____ refers to the decision-making time frame of a firm in which at least one factor of production is fixed. Costs which are fixed in the _____ have no impact on a firms decisions. For example a firm can raise output by increasing the amount of labour through overtime.
   a. 4-4-5 Calendar
   c. Long-run
   b. Short-run
   d. 529 plan

21. An _____ is a contract written by a seller that conveys to the buyer the right -- but not the obligation -- to buy (in the case of a call _____) or to sell (in the case of a put _____) a particular asset, such as a piece of property such as, among others, a futures contract. In return for granting the _____, the seller collects a payment (the premium) from the buyer.

For example, buying a call _____ provides the right to buy a specified quantity of a security at a set strike price at some time on or before expiration, while buying a put _____ provides the right to sell.

   a. AT'T Mobility LLC
   c. Annuity
   b. Amortization
   d. Option

22. In options, the _____ is a key variable in a derivatives contract between two parties. Where the contract requires delivery of the underlying instrument, the trade will be at the _____, regardless of the spot price (market price) of the underlying instrument at that time.

Definition - The fixed price at which the owner of an option can purchase, in the case of a call in the case of a put, the underlying security or commodity.

   a. Moneyness
   c. Naked put
   b. Swaption
   d. Strike price

23. In economics, collective bargaining, psychology and political science, 'free riders' are those who consume more than their fair share of a resource, or shoulder less than a fair share of the costs of its production. Free riding is usually considered to be an economic 'problem' only when it leads to the non-production or under-production of a public good (and thus to Pareto inefficiency), or when it leads to the excessive use of a common property resource. The _____ is the question of how to prevent free riding from taking place (or at least limit its negative effects) in these situations.
   a. Free rider problem
   c. 4-4-5 Calendar
   b. 7-Eleven
   d. 529 plan

Chapter 14. The Role of Financial Markets in Financial Management

1. _____ is a fee paid on borrowed assets. It is the price paid for the use of borrowed money, or, money earned by deposited funds. Assets that are sometimes lent with _____ include money, shares, consumer goods through hire purchase, major assets such as aircraft, and even entire factories in finance lease arrangements.
    a. Insolvency
    b. Interest
    c. A Random Walk Down Wall Street
    d. AAB

2. An _____ is the price a borrower pays for the use of money they do not own, and the return a lender receives for deferring the use of funds, by lending it to the borrower. _____s are normally expressed as a percentage rate over the period of one year.

    _____s targets are also a vital tool of monetary policy and are used to control variables like investment, inflation, and unemployment.

    a. Interest rate
    b. A Random Walk Down Wall Street
    c. AAB
    d. ABN Amro

3. In financial accounting, the term _____ is most commonly used to describe any part of shareholders' equity, except for basic share capital. Sometimes, the term is used instead of the term provision; such a use, however, is inconsistent with the terminology suggested by International Accounting Standards Board. For more information about provisions, see provision (accounting.)
    a. Reserve
    b. Closing entries
    c. FIFO and LIFO accounting
    d. Treasury stock

4. _____ or economic opportunity loss is the value of the next best alternative foregone as the result of making a decision. _____ analysis is an important part of a company's decision-making processes but is not treated as an actual cost in any financial statement. The next best thing that a person can engage in is referred to as the _____ of doing the best thing and ignoring the next best thing to be done.
    a. ABN Amro
    b. AAB
    c. Opportunity cost
    d. A Random Walk Down Wall Street

5. In economics, business, and accounting, a _____ is the value of money that has been used up to produce something, and hence is not available for use anymore. In business, the _____ may be one of acquisition, in which case the amount of money expended to acquire it is counted as _____. In this case, money is the input that is gone in order to acquire the thing.
    a. Sliding scale fees
    b. Fixed costs
    c. Marginal cost
    d. Cost

6.

    A _____ is a type of financial intermediary and a type of bank. Commercial banking is also known as business banking. It is a bank that provides checking accounts, savings accounts, and money market accounts and that accepts time deposits.

    a. 4-4-5 Calendar
    b. 529 plan
    c. 7-Eleven
    d. Commercial bank

Chapter 14. The Role of Financial Markets in Financial Management

7. In the United States, _____ are overnight borrowings by banks to maintain their bank reserves at the Federal Reserve. Banks keep reserves at Federal Reserve Banks to meet their reserve requirements and to clear financial transactions. Transactions in the _____ market enable depository institutions with reserve balances in excess of reserve requirements to lend reserves to institutions with reserve deficiencies.

   a. 4-4-5 Calendar
   b. Federal funds
   c. Federal funds rate
   d. Regulation T

8. In the United States, the _____ is the interest rate at which private depository institutions (mostly banks) lend balances (federal funds) at the Federal Reserve to other depository institutions, usually overnight. Changing the target rate is one form of open market operations that the Chairman of the Federal Reserve uses to regulate the supply of money in the U.S. economy.

   U.S. banks and thrift institutions are obligated by law to maintain certain levels of reserves, either as reserves with the Fed or as vault cash.

   a. Taylor rule
   b. 4-4-5 Calendar
   c. Regulation T
   d. Federal funds rate

9. _____ is a term applied in many countries to a reference interest rate used by banks. The term originally indicated the rate of interest at which banks lent to favored customers, i.e., those with high credibility, though this is no longer always the case. Some variable interest rates may be expressed as a percentage above or below _____.

   a. Reserve requirement
   b. Credit bureau
   c. Time deposit
   d. Prime rate

10. _____ or financing is to provide capital (funds), which means money for a project, a person, a business or any other private or public institutions.

    Those funds can be allocated for either short term or long term purposes. The health fund is a new way of _____ private healthcare centers.

    a. Proxy fight
    b. Product life cycle
    c. Funding
    d. Synthetic CDO

11. In economics, a _____ is a general slowdown in economic activity in a country over a sustained period of time, or a business cycle contraction. During _____s, many macroeconomic indicators vary in a similar way. Production as measured by Gross Domestic Product (GDP), employment, investment spending, capacity utilization, household incomes and business profits all fall during _____s.

    a. Fixed exchange rate
    b. Mercantilism
    c. Behavioral finance
    d. Recession

12. The _____ is the market for securities, where companies and governments can raise longterm funds. The _____ includes the stock market and the bond market. Financial regulators, such as the U.S. Securities and Exchange Commission, oversee the _____s in their designated countries to ensure that investors are protected against fraud.

    a. Forward market
    b. Spot rate
    c. Delta neutral
    d. Capital market

Chapter 14. The Role of Financial Markets in Financial Management

13. In finance, a _____ is a debt security, in which the authorized issuer owes the holders a debt and, depending on the terms of the _____, is obliged to pay interest (the coupon) and/or to repay the principal at a later date, termed maturity.

Thus a _____ is a loan: the issuer is the borrower, the _____ holder is the lender, and the coupon is the interest. _____s provide the borrower with external funds to finance long-term investments, or, in the case of government _____s, to finance current expenditure.

a. Convertible bond
b. Catastrophe bonds
c. Puttable bond
d. Bond

14. A _____ is a bond issued by a corporation. The term is usually applied to longer-term debt instruments, generally with a maturity date falling at least a year after their issue date. (The term 'commercial paper' is sometimes used for instruments with a shorter maturity.)

a. Brady bonds
b. Corporate bond
c. Government bond
d. Serial bond

15. In economics, a _____ is a mechanism that allows people to easily buy and sell (trade) financial securities (such as stocks and bonds), commodities (such as precious metals or agricultural goods), and other fungible items of value at low transaction costs and at prices that reflect the efficient-market hypothesis.

_____s have evolved significantly over several hundred years and are undergoing constant innovation to improve liquidity.

Both general markets (where many commodities are traded) and specialized markets (where only one commodity is traded) exist.

a. Cost of carry
b. Financial market
c. Delta hedging
d. Secondary market

16. _____ relates to the cost of borrowing money. It is the price that a lender charges a borrower for the use of the lender's money. _____ is different from OPEX and CAPEX, for it relates to the capital structure of a company.

a. A Random Walk Down Wall Street
b. Interest expense
c. AAB
d. ABN Amro

17. In business and accounting, _____s are everything of value that is owned by a person or company. The balance sheet of a firm records the monetary value of the _____s owned by the firm. The two major _____ classes are tangible _____s and intangible _____s.

a. EBITDA
b. Income
c. Accounts payable
d. Asset

18. A _____ is an institution, firm or individual who mediates between two or more parties in a financial context. Typically the first party is a provider of a product or service and the second party is a consumer or customer.

In the U.S., a _____ is typically an institution that facilitates the channelling of funds between lenders and borrowers indirectly.

Chapter 14. The Role of Financial Markets in Financial Management 95

a. Savings and loan association
c. Net asset value

b. Mutual fund
d. Financial intermediary

19. The _____ is the financial market where previously issued securities and financial instruments such as stock, bonds, options, and futures are bought and sold. The term '_____' is also used refer to the market for any used goods or assets, or an alternative use for an existing product or asset where the customer base is the second market

With primary issuances of securities or financial instruments, or the primary market, investors purchase these securities directly from issuers such as corporations issuing shares in an IPO or private placement, or directly from the federal government in the case of treasuries.

a. Financial market
c. Delta neutral

b. Performance attribution
d. Secondary market

20. A _____ is a fungible, negotiable instrument representing financial value. They are broadly categorized into debt securities (such as banknotes, bonds and debentures), and equity securities; e.g., common stocks. The company or other entity issuing the _____ is called the issuer.

a. Securities lending
c. Book entry

b. Tracking stock
d. Security

21. _____ is a type of private equity capital typically provided to early-stage, high-potential, growth companies in the interest of generating a return through an eventual realization event such as an IPO or trade sale of the company. _____ investments are generally made as cash in exchange for shares in the invested company. It is typical for _____ investors to identify and back companies in high technology industries such as biotechnology and ICT.

a. Tail risk
c. Treasury Inflation-Protected Securities

b. Probability distribution
d. Venture capital

22. In the United States, a _____ is an offering of securities that are not registered with the Securities and Exchange Commission (SEC.) Such offerings exploit an exemption offered by the Securities Act of 1933 that comes with several restrictions, including a prohibition against general solicitation. This exemption allows companies to avoid quarterly reporting requirements and many of the legal liabilities associated with the Sarbanes-Oxley Act.

a. 4-4-5 Calendar
c. 7-Eleven

b. 529 plan
d. Private placement

23. _____, is when a company issues common stock or shares to the public for the first time. They are often issued by smaller, younger companies seeking capital to expand, but can also be done by large privately-owned companies looking to become publicly traded.

In an _____ the issuer may obtain the assistance of an underwriting firm, which helps it determine what type of security to issue (common or preferred), best offering price and time to bring it to market.

a. Insolvency
c. Asian Financial Crisis

b. Initial public offering
d. Interest

Chapter 14. The Role of Financial Markets in Financial Management

24. A _____, in business matters, is an entity that is controlled by a bigger and more powerful entity. The controlled entity is called a company, corporation, or limited liability company, and the controlling entity is called its parent (or the parent company.) The reason for this distinction is that a lone company cannot be a _____ of any organization; only an entity representing a legal fiction as a separate entity can be a _____.
   a. Joint stock company
   b. 529 plan
   c. Subsidiary
   d. 4-4-5 Calendar

25. The term _____ or economic cycle refers to the fluctuations of economic activity (business fluctuations) around a long-term growth trend. The cycle involves shifts over time between periods of relatively rapid growth of output (recovery and prosperity), and periods of relative stagnation or decline (contraction or recession.) These fluctuations are often measured using the real gross domestic product.
   a. Fixed exchange rate
   b. Behavioral finance
   c. Deflation
   d. Business Cycle

26. The _____ is a private, nonprofit research organization dedicated to studying the science and empirics of economics, especially the American economy. It is 'committed to undertaking and disseminating unbiased economic research among public policymakers, business professionals, and the academic community.' It publishes NBER Working Papers and books. The NBER is located in Cambridge, Massachusetts with branch offices in Palo Alto, California, and New York City.
   a. National Bureau of Economic Research
   b. Microfinance
   c. General partnership
   d. National Association of State Boards of Accountancy

27. The _____ is that part of the capital markets that deals with the issuance of new securities. Companies, governments or public sector institutions can obtain funding through the sale of a new stock or bond issue. This is typically done through a syndicate of securities dealers.
   a. Primary market
   b. Peer group analysis
   c. Sector rotation
   d. Volatility clustering

28. In finance, the _____ is the global financial market for short-term borrowing and lending. It provides short-term liquidity funding for the global financial system. The _____ is where short-term obligations such as Treasury bills, commercial paper and bankers' acceptances are bought and sold.
   a. Cramdown
   b. Debt-for-equity swap
   c. Consumer debt
   d. Money market

29. The _____ is a stock exchange based in New York City, New York. It is the largest stock exchange in the world by dollar value of its listed companies securities. As of October 2008, the combined capitalization of all domestic _____ listed companies was $10.1 trillion.
   a. 4-4-5 Calendar
   b. 7-Eleven
   c. 529 plan
   d. New York Stock Exchange

30. A _____, securities exchange or (in Europe) bourse is a corporation or mutual organization which provides 'trading' facilities for stock brokers and traders, to trade stocks and other securities. _____s also provide facilities for the issue and redemption of securities as well as other financial instruments and capital events including the payment of income and dividends. The securities traded on a _____ include: shares issued by companies, unit trusts and other pooled investment products and bonds.

Chapter 14. The Role of Financial Markets in Financial Management

a. Stock Exchange
b. 7-Eleven
c. 4-4-5 Calendar
d. 529 plan

31. A _____ is the highest price that a buyer (i.e., bidder) is willing to pay for a good. It is usually referred to simply as the 'bid.'

In bid and ask, the _____ stands in contrast to the ask price or 'offer', and the difference between the two is called the bid/ask spread.

An unsolicited bid or offer is when a person or company receives a bid even though they are not looking to sell.

a. Settlement date
b. Mid price
c. Political risk
d. Bid price

32. A _____ is a company or other organization that trades securities for its own account or on behalf of its customers.

When executing trade orders on behalf of a customer, the institution is said to be acting as a broker. When executing trades for its own account, the institution is said to be acting as a 'dealer.' Securities bought from clients or other firms in the capacity of dealer may be sold to clients or other firms acting again in the capacity of dealer, or they may become a part of the firm's holdings.

a. Person-to-person lending
b. Broker-dealer
c. Trust company
d. Mutual fund

33. The _____ is an American stock exchange. It is the largest electronic screen-based equity securities trading market in the United States. With approximately 3,200 companies, it has more trading volume per day than any other stock exchange in the world.

a. 529 plan
b. 4-4-5 Calendar
c. 7-Eleven
d. NASDAQ

34. The _____ of 1933 established the Federal Deposit Insurance Corporation (FDIC) in the United States and included banking reforms, some of which were designed to control speculation. Some provisions such as Regulation Q, which allowed the Federal Reserve to regulate interest rates in savings accounts, were repealed by the Depository Institutions Deregulation and Monetary Control Act of 1980. Provisions that prohibit a bank holding company from owning other financial companies were repealed on November 12, 1999, by the Gramm-Leach-Bliley Act.

a. 4-4-5 Calendar
b. 529 plan
c. 7-Eleven
d. Glass-Steagall Act

35. The _____ Act is an Act of the 106th United States Congress which repealed part of the Glass-Steagall Act of 1933, opening up competition among banks, securities companies and insurance companies. The Glass-Steagall Act prohibited any one institution from acting as both an investment bank and a commercial bank, or as both a bank and an insurer.

The _____ Act (GLBA) allowed commercial and investment banks to consolidate.

Chapter 14. The Role of Financial Markets in Financial Management

a. 7-Eleven
b. Gramm-Leach-Bliley
c. 529 plan
d. 4-4-5 Calendar

36. A _____ or bank is a financial institution whose primary activity is to act as a payment agent for customers and to borrow and lend money.

The first modern bank was founded in Italy in Genoa in 1406, its name was Banco di San Giorgio (Bank of St. George.)

Many other financial activities were added over time.

a. Bought deal
b. 4-4-5 Calendar
c. Banker
d. Black Sea Trade and Development Bank

37. A _____, in its most general sense, is a solemn promise to engage in or refrain from a specified action.

More specifically, a _____, in contrast to a contract, is a one-way agreement whereby the _____er is the only party bound by the promise. A _____ may have conditions and prerequisites that qualify the undertaking, including the actions of second or third parties, but there is no inherent agreement by such other parties to fulfill those requirements.

a. Partnership
b. Federal Trade Commission Act
c. Clayton Antitrust Act
d. Covenant

38. A _____ is a state law in the United States that regulates the offering and sale of securities to protect the public from fraud. Though the specific provisions of these laws vary among states, they all require the registration of all securities offerings and sales, as well as of stock brokers and brokerage firms. Each state's _____ is administered by its appropriate regulatory agency, and most also provide private causes of action for private investors who have been injured by securities fraud.

a. Court of Audit of Belgium
b. Patent
c. Bundesrechnungshof
d. Blue sky law

39. Congress enacted the _____, in the aftermath of the stock market crash of 1929 and during the ensuing Great Depression. It requires that any offer or sale of securities using the means and instrumentalities of interstate commerce be registered pursuant to the 1933 Act, unless an exemption from registration exists under the law.

a. 7-Eleven
b. 529 plan
c. 4-4-5 Calendar
d. Securities Act of 1933

40. _____ is the trading of a corporation's stock or other securities (e.g. bonds or stock options) by individuals with potential access to non-public information about the company. In most countries, trading by corporate insiders such as officers, key employees, directors, and large shareholders may be legal, if this trading is done in a way that does not take advantage of non-public information. However, the term is frequently used to refer to a practice in which an insider or a related party trades based on material non-public information obtained during the performance of the insider's duties at the corporation, or otherwise in breach of a fiduciary duty or other relationship of trust and confidence or where the non-public information was misappropriated from the company.

Chapter 14. The Role of Financial Markets in Financial Management

a. Open outcry
c. Intellidex
b. Equity investment
d. Insider trading

41. The _____ of 1934 is a law governing the secondary trading of securities (stocks, bonds, and debentures) in the United States of America. The Act, 48 Stat. 881 (enacted June 6, 1934), codified at 15 U.S.C. § 78a et seq., was a sweeping piece of legislation. The Act and related statutes form the basis of regulation of the financial markets and their participants in the United States.
   a. 7-Eleven
   c. 4-4-5 Calendar
   b. Securities Exchange Act
   d. 529 plan

42. The U.S. _____ is an independent agency of the United States government which holds primary responsibility for enforcing the federal securities laws and regulating the securities industry, the nation's stock and options exchanges, and other electronic securities markets. The SEC was created by section 4 of the SEC of 1934 (now codified as 15 U.S.C. § 78d and commonly referred to as the 1934 Act.)
   a. 4-4-5 Calendar
   c. 7-Eleven
   b. 529 plan
   d. Securities and Exchange Commission

43. _____ is an expansion of accounting rules that goes beyond the realm of financial measures for both individual economic entities and national economies. It is advocated by those who consider the focus of the present standards and practices wholly inadequate to the task of measuring and reporting the activity, success, and failure of modern enterprise, including government.

Real debate concerns concepts such as whether to report transactions, such as asset acquisitions, at their cost or at their current market values.

   a. AAB
   c. A Random Walk Down Wall Street
   b. Accounting Reform
   d. Inflation targeting

44. The term _____ usually refers to a company that is permitted to offer its registered securities for sale to the general public, typically through a stock exchange, or occasionally a company whose stock is traded over the counter via market makers who use non-exchange quotation services.

The term '_____' may also refer to a company owned by the government.

   a. Corporation
   c. First Prudential Markets
   b. General partnership
   d. Public Company

45. The _____ (sometimes called 'Peekaboo') is a private-sector, non-profit corporation created by the Sarbanes-Oxley Act, a 2002 United States federal law, to oversee the auditors of public companies. Its stated purpose is to 'protect the interests of investors and further the public interest in the preparation of informative, fair, and independent audit reports'. Although a private entity, the _____ has many government-like regulatory functions, making it in some ways similar to the private Self Regulatory Organizations (SROs) that regulate stock markets and other aspects of the financial markets in the United States.
   a. World Trade Organization
   c. Financial Crimes Enforcement Network
   b. Gamelan Council
   d. Public Company Accounting Oversight Board

Chapter 14. The Role of Financial Markets in Financial Management

46. In finance, the _____ between two currencies specifies how much one currency is worth in terms of the other. For example an _____ of 102 Japanese yen to the United States dollar means that JPY 102 is worth the same as USD 1. The foreign exchange market is one of the largest markets in the world.

   a. A Random Walk Down Wall Street
   b. ABN Amro
   c. AAB
   d. Exchange rate

47. _____ is a form of risk that arises from the change in price of one currency against another. Whenever investors or companies have assets or business operations across national borders, they face _____ if their positions are not hedged.

   - Transaction risk is the risk that exchange rates will change unfavourably over time. It can be hedged against using forward currency contracts;
   - Translation risk is an accounting risk, proportional to the amount of assets held in foreign currencies. Changes in the exchange rate over time will render a report inaccurate, and so assets are usually balanced by borrowings in that currency.

   The exchange risk associated with a foreign denominated instrument is a key element in foreign investment. This risk flows from differential monetary policy and growth in real productivity, which results in differential inflation rates.

   a. Credit risk
   b. Tracking error
   c. Market risk
   d. Currency risk

48. _____ are securities that can be easily converted into cash. Such securities will generally have highly liquid markets allowing the security to be sold at a reasonable price very quickly. This is a usual feature in real estate.

   a. Tracking stock
   b. Securities lending
   c. Book entry
   d. Marketable

49. The '_____' is approximately the nominal interest rate minus the inflation rate Since the inflation rate over the course of a loan is not known initially, volatility in inflation represents a risk to both the lender and the borrower.

   In economics and finance, an individual who lends money for repayment at a later point in time expects to be compensated for the time value of money, or not having the use of that money while it is lent.

   a. 4-4-5 Calendar
   b. 529 plan
   c. 7-Eleven
   d. Real interest rate

Chapter 15. Analysis and Impact of Leverage

1. _____ is normally any risk associated with any form of financing.

Depending on the nature of the investment, the type of 'investment' risk will vary. High risk investments have greater potential rewards, but you may lose your money instead by taking the risk for more money.

- a. Revaluation
- b. Liquidating dividend
- c. Stock market index option
- d. Financial risk

2. In financial and business accounting, _____ is a measure of a firm's profitability that excludes interest and income tax expenses.

EBIT = Operating Revenue - Operating Expenses (OPEX) + Non-operating Income

Operating Income = Operating Revenue - Operating Expenses

Operating income is the difference between operating revenues and operating expenses, but it is also sometimes used as a synonym for EBIT and operating profit. This is true if the firm has no non-operating income.

- a. AAB
- b. A Random Walk Down Wall Street
- c. ABN Amro
- d. Earnings before interest and taxes

3. In finance, _____ (or gearing) is borrowing money to supplement existing funds for investment in such a way that the potential positive or negative outcome is magnified and/or enhanced. It generally refers to using borrowed funds, or debt, so as to attempt to increase the returns to equity. Deleveraging is the action of reducing borrowings.

- a. Financial endowment
- b. Pension fund
- c. Leverage
- d. Limited partnership

4. The _____ is a measure of how revenue growth translates into growth in operating income. It is a measure of leverage, and of how risky (volatile) a company's operating income is.

There are various measures of _____, which can be interpreted analogously to financial leverage.

- a. Asset turnover
- b. Average accounting return
- c. Invested capital
- d. Operating leverage

5. _____ in finance is a risk management technique, related to hedging, that mixes a wide variety of investments within a portfolio. Because the fluctuations of a single security have less impact on a diverse portfolio, _____ minimizes the risk from any one investment.

A simple example of _____ is the following: On a particular island the entire economy consists of two companies: one that sells umbrellas and another that sells sunscreen.

- a. Diversification
- b. 4-4-5 Calendar
- c. 7-Eleven
- d. 529 plan

Chapter 15. Analysis and Impact of Leverage

6. In economics and business, specifically cost accounting, the _____ is the point at which cost or expenses and revenue are equal: there is no net loss or gain, and one has 'broken even'. A profit or a loss has not been made, although opportunity costs have been paid, and capital has received the risk-adjusted, expected return.

For example, if the business sells less than 200 tables each month, it will make a loss, if it sells more, it will be a profit.

   a. Market microstructure   b. Defined contribution plan
   c. Break-even point   d. Fixed asset turnover

7. A _____ is an expenditure creating future benefits. A _____ is incurred when a business spends money either to buy fixed assets or to add to the value of an existing fixed asset with a useful life that extends beyond the taxable year. Capex are used by a company to acquire or upgrade physical assets such as equipment, property, or industrial buildings.

   a. Capital expenditure   b. Cost of capital
   c. Weighted average cost of capital   d. 4-4-5 Calendar

8. In economics, business, and accounting, a _____ is the value of money that has been used up to produce something, and hence is not available for use anymore. In business, the _____ may be one of acquisition, in which case the amount of money expended to acquire it is counted as _____. In this case, money is the input that is gone in order to acquire the thing.

   a. Sliding scale fees   b. Marginal cost
   c. Fixed costs   d. Cost

9. _____ are business expenses that are not dependent on the level of production or sales. They tend to be time-related, such as salaries or rents being paid per month. This is in contrast to Variable costs, which are volume-related (and are paid per quantity.)

   a. Transaction cost   b. Sliding scale fees
   c. Fixed costs   d. Marginal cost

10. _____ are costs that are not directly accountable to a particular function or product. _____ may be either fixed or variable. _____ include taxes, administration, personnel and security costs, and are also known as overhead.

   a. A Random Walk Down Wall Street   b. Equivalent annual cost
   c. AAB   d. Indirect costs

11. _____ are expenses that change in proportion to the activity of a business. In other words, _____ are the sum of marginal costs. It can also be considered normal costs. Along with fixed costs, _____ make up the two components of total cost. Direct Costs, however, are costs that can be associated with a particular cost object.

   a. Fixed costs   b. Cost accounting
   c. Transaction cost   d. Variable costs

12. _____ is the total money received from the sale of any given quantity of output.

The _____ is calculated by taking the price of the sale times the quantity sold, i.e.

Chapter 15. Analysis and Impact of Leverage

_____ = price X quantity.

a. Defined contribution plan
b. Total revenue
c. Fixed asset turnover
d. Break-even point

13. In business, _____ is income that a company receives from its normal business activities, usually from the sale of goods and services to customers. Some companies also receive _____ from interest, dividends or royalties paid to them by other companies. _____ may refer to business income in general, or it may refer to the amount, in a monetary unit, received during a period of time, as in 'Last year, Company X had _____ of $32 million.'

In many countries, including the UK, _____ is referred to as turnover.

a. Matching principle
b. Furniture, Fixtures and Equipment
c. Revenue
d. Bottom line

14. In cost-volume-profit analysis, a form of management accounting, _____ is the marginal profit per unit sale. It is a useful quantity in carrying out various calculations, and can be used as a measure of operating leverage.

The Total _____ is Total Revenue (TR, or Sales) minus Total Variable Cost (TVC):

TContribution margin = TR >− TVC

The Unit _____ (C) is Unit Revenue (Price, P) minus Unit Variable Cost (V):

C = P >− V

The _____ Ratio is the percentage of Contribution over Total Revenue, which can be calculated from the unit contribution over unit price or total contribution over Total Revenue:

For instance, if the price is $10 and the unit variable cost is $2, then the unit _____ is $8, and the _____ ratio is $8/$10 = 80%.

a. Contribution margin
b. 7-Eleven
c. 4-4-5 Calendar
d. 529 plan

103

Chapter 15. Analysis and Impact of Leverage

15. In finance, a _____ is collateral that the holder of a position in securities, options, or futures contracts has to deposit to cover the credit risk of his counterparty (most often his broker.) This risk can arise if the holder has done any of the following:

- borrowed cash from the counterparty to buy securities or options,
- sold securities or options short, or
- entered into a futures contract.

The collateral can be in the form of cash or securities, and it is deposited in a _____ account. On U.S. futures exchanges, '_____' was formally called performance bond.

_____ buying is buying securities with cash borrowed from a broker, using other securities as collateral.

a. Procter ' Gamble
c. Margin
b. Share
d. Credit

16. _____, refers to consumption opportunity gained by an entity within a specified time frame, which is generally expressed in monetary terms. However, for households and individuals, '_____ is the sum of all the wages, salaries, profits, interests payments, rents and other forms of earnings received... in a given period of time.' For firms, _____ generally refers to net-profit: what remains of revenue after expenses have been subtracted.

a. OIBDA
c. Annual report
b. Income
d. Accrual

17. An _____ is a financial statement for companies that indicates how Revenue is transformed into net income The purpose of the _____ is to show managers and investors whether the company made or lost money during the period being reported.

The important thing to remember about an _____ is that it represents a period of time.

a. A Random Walk Down Wall Street
c. ABN Amro
b. AAB
d. Income statement

18. _____ is a term used in accounting, economics and finance to spread the cost of an asset over the span of several years.

In simple words we can say that _____ is the reduction in the value of an asset due to usage, passage of time, wear and tear, technological outdating or obsolescence, depletion or other such factors.

In accounting, _____ is a term used to describe any method of attributing the historical or purchase cost of an asset across its useful life, roughly corresponding to normal wear and tear.

a. Matching principle
c. Bottom line
b. Deferred financing costs
d. Depreciation

19. _____ or financing is to provide capital (funds), which means money for a project, a person, a business or any other private or public institutions.

Those funds can be allocated for either short term or long term purposes. The health fund is a new way of _____ private healthcare centers.

a. Synthetic CDO
b. Proxy fight
c. Product life cycle
d. Funding

Chapter 16. Planning the Firm's Financing Mix

1. In finance, _____ refers to the way a corporation finances its assets through some combination of equity, debt, or hybrid securities. A firm's _____ is then the composition or 'structure' of its liabilities. For example, a firm that sells $20 billion in equity and $80 billion in debt is said to be 20% equity-financed and 80% debt-financed.
   a. Rights issue
   b. Capital structure
   c. Book building
   d. Market for corporate control

2. _____ is an area of finance dealing with the financial decisions corporations make and the tools and analysis used to make these decisions. The primary goal of _____ is to maximize corporate value while managing the firm's financial risks. Although it is in principle different from managerial finance which studies the financial decisions of all firms, rather than corporations alone, the main concepts in the study of _____ are applicable to the financial problems of all kinds of firms.
   a. Special purpose entity
   b. Cash flow
   c. Corporate finance
   d. Gross profit

3. _____ is that which is owed; usually referencing assets owed, but the term can cover other obligations. In the case of assets, _____ is a means of using future purchasing power in the present before a summation has been earned. Some companies and corporations use _____ as a part of their overall corporate finance strategy.
   a. Cross-collateralization
   b. Partial Payment
   c. Credit cycle
   d. Debt

4. In economics, business, and accounting, a _____ is the value of money that has been used up to produce something, and hence is not available for use anymore. In business, the _____ may be one of acquisition, in which case the amount of money expended to acquire it is counted as _____. In this case, money is the input that is gone in order to acquire the thing.
   a. Marginal cost
   b. Sliding scale fees
   c. Cost
   d. Fixed costs

5. _____, refers to consumption opportunity gained by an entity within a specified time frame, which is generally expressed in monetary terms. However, for households and individuals, '_____ is the sum of all the wages, salaries, profits, interests payments, rents and other forms of earnings received... in a given period of time.' For firms, _____ generally refers to net-profit: what remains of revenue after expenses have been subtracted.
   a. Accrual
   b. Annual report
   c. OIBDA
   d. Income

6. _____ is the difference between operating revenues and operating expenses, but it is also sometimes used as a synonym for EBIT and operating profit. This is true if the firm has no non-_____.

A professional investor contemplating a change to the capital structure of a firm (e.g., through a leveraged buyout) first evaluates a firm's fundamental earnings potential (reflected by Earnings Before Interest, Taxes, Depreciation and Amortization EBITDA and EBIT), and then determines the optimal use of debt vs. equity.

   a. AAB
   b. A Random Walk Down Wall Street
   c. Operating income
   d. ABN Amro

7. In finance, _____ is the process of estimating the potential market value of a financial asset or liability. they can be done on assets (for example, investments in marketable securities such as stocks, options, business enterprises, or intangible assets such as patents and trademarks) or on liabilities (e.g., Bonds issued by a company.) _____s are required in many contexts including investment analysis, capital budgeting, merger and acquisition transactions, financial reporting, taxable events to determine the proper tax liability, and in litigation.
    a. Procter ' Gamble
    b. Margin
    c. Share
    d. Valuation

Chapter 16. Planning the Firm`s Financing Mix

8. Briggs could refer to:

   - Briggs cliff, a fictional place in Fullmetal Alchemist manga
   - Briggs (crater), a lunar crater
   - Briggs Initiative, either of two pieces of Californian legislation sponsored by John Briggs
   - Briggs Islet, Tasmania, Australia
   - Briggs, Oklahoma, USA
   - Briggs, Texas, USA
   - _____, a manufacturer of air-cooled gasoline engines
   - The Briggs - a punk rock band
   - Myers-Briggs Type Indicator

   - Anne Briggs, English folk singer
   - Ansel Briggs, American politician
   - Arthur E. Briggs, California politician
   - Asa Briggs, British historian
   - Barbara Briggs, American dramatist
   - Barbara G. Briggs, Australian botanist
   - Barry Briggs, New Zealand World Motorcycle speedway champion
   - Barry Bruce-Briggs, public policy writer
   - Benjamin Briggs, captain of the Mary Celeste
   - Bill Briggs, American skier
   - Billy Briggs, American musician
   - Bobby Briggs, fictional character from Twin Peaks
   - Charles Augustus Briggs, American theologian
   - Charles Frederick Briggs, American journalist
   - Clare Briggs, American comics artist
   - David Briggs:
     - David Briggs (producer) (1944-1995), American record producer
     - David Briggs (composer) English organist and composer
     - David Briggs (Australian musician), guitarist with Little River Band and Australian record producer
   - Derek Briggs, Irish paleontologist
   - Everett Francis Briggs, (1908-2006), American Catholic priest
   - Frank A. Briggs, American politician
   - Frank O. Briggs, American politician
   - Frank P. Briggs, American politician
   - Gary Briggs (musician), British guitarist
   - Gary Briggs (footballer), British footballer
   - George N. Briggs, American politician
   - Major Garland Briggs, fictional character from Twin Peaks
   - Harold Briggs
     - Harold Briggs (General), British general
     - Harold Briggs (politician), British Conservative MP
   - Henry Briggs (politician)
   - Henry Briggs (mathematician), English mathematician
   - Hortense Briggs, fictional character from An American Tragedy by Theodore Dreiser
   - Ian Briggs, television writer
   - Jack Briggs, American instrument maker
   - James Briggs, any of several people
   - Jason W. Briggs, American Latter Day Saint leader
   - Jeff Briggs, American composer and former computer games executive
   - Joe Bob Briggs, pseudonym of John Irving Bloom, film critic and actor
   - John Briggs (politician), a California politician
   - John Briggs (author)
   - Johnny Briggs:

- - Johnny Briggs (cricketer)
  - Johnny Briggs (actor), actor who played Mike Baldwin on the British soap opera Coronation Street
  - Johnny Briggs (baseball), a former Major League Baseball outfielder
- Jon Briggs, British radio personality
- Jonny Briggs, BBC children's television programme first broadcast in 1985.
- Karen Briggs, American violinist
- Katharine Cook Briggs, co-inventor of the Myers-Briggs Type Indicator personality test
- Katharine Mary Briggs, British author
- Kevin 'She'kspere' Briggs, American record producer
- Lance Briggs, American football player
- LeBaron Russell Briggs, American educator
- Luke Briggs, British Steward
- Lyman James Briggs, American physicist and civil servant
- Matilda Briggs, passenger on the Marie Celeste
- Matthew Briggs, English footballer
- Nicholas Briggs, British actor
- Nigel Briggs, Singer/Song writer
- Patricia Briggs, American fantasy writer
- Paul Briggs, Australian boxer
- Raymond Briggs, British illustrator and author
- Sandra Briggs, fictional character from Emmerdale
- Shannon Briggs, American boxer
- Stephen Briggs, British Discworld adapter
- Stephen Foster Briggs, American engineer, co-founder of The _____ Company
- Ted Briggs, British seaman
- Tom Briggs, American football player
- Walter Briggs, Major League Baseball owner

Chapter 16. Planning the Firm's Financing Mix

    a. 529 plan
    b. 4-4-5 Calendar
    c. 7-Eleven
    d. Briggs ' Stratton

9. The _____ is an expected return that the provider of capital plans to earn on their investment.

Capital (money) used for funding a business should earn returns for the capital providers who risk their capital. For an investment to be worthwhile, the expected return on capital must be greater than the _____.

    a. 4-4-5 Calendar
    b. Capital intensity
    c. Cost of capital
    d. Weighted average cost of capital

10. _____ is equal to the income that a firm has after subtracting costs and expenses from the total revenue. _____ can be distributed among holders of common stock as a dividend or held by the firm as retained earnings. _____ is an accounting term; in some countries (such as the UK) profit is the usual term.

    a. Write-off
    b. Furniture, Fixtures and Equipment
    c. Net income
    d. Historical cost

11. The _____ is a stock exchange based in New York City, New York. It is the largest stock exchange in the world by dollar value of its listed companies securities. As of October 2008, the combined capitalization of all domestic _____ listed companies was $10.1 trillion.

    a. 7-Eleven
    b. 529 plan
    c. 4-4-5 Calendar
    d. New York Stock Exchange

12. A _____, securities exchange or (in Europe) bourse is a corporation or mutual organization which provides 'trading' facilities for stock brokers and traders, to trade stocks and other securities. _____s also provide facilities for the issue and redemption of securities as well as other financial instruments and capital events including the payment of income and dividends. The securities traded on a _____ include: shares issued by companies, unit trusts and other pooled investment products and bonds.

    a. 7-Eleven
    b. 4-4-5 Calendar
    c. 529 plan
    d. Stock Exchange

13. In finance, _____ (or gearing) is borrowing money to supplement existing funds for investment in such a way that the potential positive or negative outcome is magnified and/or enhanced. It generally refers to using borrowed funds, or debt, so as to attempt to increase the returns to equity. Deleveraging is the action of reducing borrowings.

    a. Financial endowment
    b. Limited partnership
    c. Pension fund
    d. Leverage

14. The _____ is a measure of how revenue growth translates into growth in operating income. It is a measure of leverage, and of how risky (volatile) a company's operating income is.

There are various measures of _____, which can be interpreted analogously to financial leverage.

    a. Asset turnover
    b. Average accounting return
    c. Invested capital
    d. Operating leverage

Chapter 16. Planning the Firm's Financing Mix

15. _____ is a fee paid on borrowed assets. It is the price paid for the use of borrowed money, or, money earned by deposited funds. Assets that are sometimes lent with _____ include money, shares, consumer goods through hire purchase, major assets such as aircraft, and even entire factories in finance lease arrangements.
    a. Insolvency
    b. Interest
    c. AAB
    d. A Random Walk Down Wall Street

16. _____ relates to the cost of borrowing money. It is the price that a lender charges a borrower for the use of the lender's money. _____ is different from OPEX and CAPEX, for it relates to the capital structure of a company.
    a. ABN Amro
    b. Interest expense
    c. A Random Walk Down Wall Street
    d. AAB

17. A _____ is the reduction in income taxes that results from taking an allowable deduction from taxable income. For example, because interest on debt is a tax-deductible expense, taking on debt creates a _____. Since a _____ is a way to save cash flows, it increases the value of the business, and it is an important aspect of business valuation.
    a. Refinancing risk
    b. Tax shield
    c. Present value of costs
    d. Present value of benefits

18. An _____ is an economic concept that relates to the cost incurred by an entity (such as organizations) associated with problems such as divergent management-shareholder objectives and information asymmetry. The costs consist of two main sources:

    1. The costs inherently associated with using an agent (e.g., the risk that agents will use organizational resource for their own benefit) and
    2. The costs of techniques used to mitigate the problems associated with using an agent (e.g., the costs of producing financial statements or the use of stock options to align executive interests to shareholder interests.)

    Though effects of _____ are present in any agency relationship, the term is most used in business contexts.

    The information asymmetry that exists between shareholders and the Chief Executive Officer is generally considered to be a classic example of a principal-agent problem. The agent (the manager) is working on behalf of the principal (the shareholders), who does not observe the actions of the agent.

    a. Agency cost
    b. ABN Amro
    c. A Random Walk Down Wall Street
    d. AAB

19. In political science and economics, the _____ or agency dilemma treats the difficulties that arise under conditions of incomplete and asymmetric information when a principal hires an agent. Various mechanisms may be used to try to align the interests of the agent with those of the principal, such as piece rates/commissions, profit sharing, efficiency wages, performance measurement (including financial statements), the agent posting a bond, or fear of firing. The _____ is found in most employer/employee relationships, for example, when stockholders hire top executives of corporations.
    a. 4-4-5 Calendar
    b. 529 plan
    c. 7-Eleven
    d. Principal-agent problem

Chapter 16. Planning the Firm's Financing Mix

20. A _____ is an international bond that is denominated in a currency not native to the country where it is issued. It can be categorised according to the currency in which it is issued. London is one of the centers of the _____ market, but _____s may be traded throughout the world - for example in Singapore or Tokyo.
   a. Economic entity
   b. Interest rate option
   c. Education production function
   d. Eurobond

21. In finance, a _____ is a debt security, in which the authorized issuer owes the holders a debt and, depending on the terms of the _____, is obliged to pay interest (the coupon) and/or to repay the principal at a later date, termed maturity.

   Thus a _____ is a loan: the issuer is the borrower, the _____ holder is the lender, and the coupon is the interest. _____s provide the borrower with external funds to finance long-term investments, or, in the case of government _____s, to finance current expenditure.

   a. Convertible bond
   b. Puttable bond
   c. Catastrophe bonds
   d. Bond

22. A _____, in its most general sense, is a solemn promise to engage in or refrain from a specified action.

   More specifically, a _____, in contrast to a contract, is a one-way agreement whereby the _____er is the only party bound by the promise. A _____ may have conditions and prerequisites that qualify the undertaking, including the actions of second or third parties, but there is no inherent agreement by such other parties to fulfill those requirements.

   a. Clayton Antitrust Act
   b. Covenant
   c. Federal Trade Commission Act
   d. Partnership

23. A _____ is a situation that involves losing one quality or aspect of something in return for gaining another quality or aspect. It implies a decision to be made with full comprehension of both the upside and downside of a particular choice.

   In economics the term is expressed as opportunity cost, referring the most preferred alternative given up.

   a. Capital outflow
   b. Total revenue
   c. Break-even point
   d. Trade-off

24. The _____ of Capital Structure refers to the idea that a company chooses how much debt finance and how much equity finance to use by balancing the costs and benefits. The classical version of the hypothesis goes back to Kraus and Litzenberger who considered a balance between the dead-weight costs of bankruptcy and the tax saving benefits of debt. Often agency costs are also included in the balance.
   a. Trade-off theory
   b. Firm commitment
   c. Rights issue
   d. Financial distress

Chapter 16. Planning the Firm's Financing Mix

25. In the theory of firm's capital structure and financing decisions, the _____ or Pecking Order Model was developed by Stewart C. Myers and Nicolas Majluf in 1984. It states that companies prioritize their sources of financing (from internal financing to equity) according to the law of least effort, or of least resistance, preferring to raise equity as a financing means of last resort. Hence, internal funds are used first, and when that is depleted, debt is issued, and when it is not sensible to issue any more debt, equity is issued.

   a. 529 plan
   b. 4-4-5 Calendar
   c. The Dogs of the Dow
   d. Pecking order theory

26. In corporate finance, _____ is a cash flow available for distribution among all the security holders of a company. They include equity holders, debt holders, preferred stock holders, convertible security holders, and so on.

Note that the first three lines above are calculated for you on the standard Statement of Cash Flows.

   a. Safety stock
   b. Forfaiting
   c. Funding
   d. Free cash flow

27. _____ is the balance of the amounts of cash being received and paid by a business during a defined period of time, sometimes tied to a specific project. Measurement of _____ can be used

   - to evaluate the state or performance of a business or project.
   - to determine problems with liquidity. Being profitable does not necessarily mean being liquid. A company can fail because of a shortage of cash, even while profitable.
   - to generate project rate of returns. The time of _____s into and out of projects are used as inputs to financial models such as internal rate of return, and net present value.
   - to examine income or growth of a business when it is believed that accrual accounting concepts do not represent economic realities. Alternately, _____ can be used to 'validate' the net income generated by accrual accounting.

_____ as a generic term may be used differently depending on context, and certain _____ definitions may be adapted by analysts and users for their own uses. Common terms include operating _____ and free _____.

_____s can be classified into:

1. Operational _____s: Cash received or expended as a result of the company's core business activities.
2. Investment _____s: Cash received or expended through capital expenditure, investments or acquisitions.
3. Financing _____s: Cash received or expended as a result of financial activities, such as interests and dividends.

All three together - the net _____ - are necessary to reconcile the beginning cash balance to the ending cash balance. Loan draw downs or equity injections, that is just shifting of capital but no expenditure as such, are not considered in the net _____.

Chapter 16. Planning the Firm's Financing Mix

a. Corporate finance
c. Shareholder value
b. Cash flow
d. Real option

28. _____ or financing is to provide capital (funds), which means money for a project, a person, a business or any other private or public institutions.

Those funds can be allocated for either short term or long term purposes. The health fund is a new way of _____ private healthcare centers.

a. Synthetic CDO
c. Product life cycle
b. Proxy fight
d. Funding

29. A _____ occurs when a financial sponsor acquires a controlling interest in a company's equity and where a significant percentage of the purchase price is financed through leverage (borrowing.) The assets of the acquired company are used as collateral for the borrowed capital, sometimes with assets of the acquiring company. The bonds or other paper issued for _____s are commonly considered not to be investment grade because of the significant risks involved.

a. Limited partnership
c. Pension fund
b. Leverage
d. Leveraged buyout

30. A _____ is a fund established by a government agency or business for the purpose of reducing debt.

The _____ was first used in Great Britain in the 18th century to reduce national debt. While used by Robert Walpole in 1716 and effectively in the 1720s and early 1730s, it originated in the commercial tax syndicates of the Italian peninsula of the 14th century to retire redeemable public debt of those cities.

a. Sinking fund
c. Security interest
b. Debtor
d. Modern portfolio theory

31. _____ are the earnings returned on the initial investment amount.

In the US, the Financial Accounting Standards Board (FASB) requires companies' income statements to report _____ for each of the major categories of the income statement: continuing operations, discontinued operations, extraordinary items, and net income.

The _____ formula does not include preferred dividends for categories outside of continued operations and net income.

a. Inventory turnover
c. Average accounting return
b. Assets turnover
d. Earnings per share

32. In business and finance, a _____ (also referred to as equity _____) of stock means a _____ of ownership in a corporation (company.) In the plural, stocks is often used as a synonym for _____s especially in the United States, but it is less commonly used that way outside of North America.

In the United Kingdom, South Africa, and Australia, stock can also refer to completely different financial instruments such as government bonds or, less commonly, to all kinds of marketable securities.

a. Share
b. Margin
c. Procter ' Gamble
d. Bucket shop

33. In financial accounting, a _____ or statement of financial position is a summary of a person's or organization's balances. Assets, liabilities and ownership equity are listed as of a specific date, such as the end of its financial year. A _____ is often described as a snapshot of a company's financial condition.

a. Statement of retained earnings
b. Financial statements
c. Statement on Auditing Standards No. 70: Service Organizations
d. Balance sheet

34. In finance, a _____ or accounting ratio is a ratio of two selected numerical values taken from an enterprise's financial statements. There are many standard ratios used to try to evaluate the overall financial condition of a corporation or other organization. They may be used by managers within a firm, by current and potential shareholders (owners) of a firm, and by a firm's creditors. Security analysts use these to compare the strengths and weaknesses in various companies.

a. Sustainable growth rate
b. Financial ratio
c. Return on capital employed
d. Price/cash flow ratio

35. In economic models, the _____ time frame assumes no fixed factors of production. Firms can enter or leave the marketplace, and the cost (and availability) of land, labor, raw materials, and capital goods can be assumed to vary. In contrast, in the short-run time frame, certain factors are assumed to be fixed, because there is not sufficient time for them to change.

a. 4-4-5 Calendar
b. Short-run
c. Long-run
d. 529 plan

36. _____ or interest coverage ratio is a measure of a company's ability to honor its debt payments. It may be calculated as either EBIT or EBITDA divided by the total interest payable.

$$\text{Times-Interest-Earned} = \frac{\text{EBIT or EBITDA}}{\text{Interest Charges}}$$

- Financial ratio
- Financial leverage
- EBIT
- EBITDA
- Debt service coverage ratio

Interest Charges = Traditionally 'charges' refers to interest expense found on the income statement.

_____ or Interest Coverage is a great tool when measuring a company's ability to meet its debt obligations.

a. Return of capital
c. Net assets
b. Cash conversion cycle
d. Times interest earned

37. In business, _____ is the total assets minus total outside liabilities of an individual or a company. For a company, this is called shareholders' equity and may be referred to as book value. _____ is stated as at a particular point in time.
   a. Net worth
   b. Moneylender
   c. Certified International Investment Analyst
   d. Restructuring

38. _____ is the planning process used to determine whether a firm's long term investments such as new machinery, replacement machinery, new plants, new products, and research development projects are worth pursuing. It is budget for major capital, or investment, expenditures.

Many formal methods are used in _____, including the techniques such as

- Net present value
- Profitability index
- Internal rate of return
- Modified Internal Rate of Return
- Equivalent annuity

These methods use the incremental cash flows from each potential investment, or project. Techniques based on accounting earnings and accounting rules are sometimes used - though economists consider this to be improper - such as the accounting rate of return, and 'return on investment.' Simplified and hybrid methods are used as well, such as payback period and discounted payback period.

   a. Shareholder value
   b. Capital budgeting
   c. Preferred stock
   d. Financial distress

39. _____ is a form of risk that arises from the change in price of one currency against another. Whenever investors or companies have assets or business operations across national borders, they face _____ if their positions are not hedged.

- Transaction risk is the risk that exchange rates will change unfavourably over time. It can be hedged against using forward currency contracts;
- Translation risk is an accounting risk, proportional to the amount of assets held in foreign currencies. Changes in the exchange rate over time will render a report inaccurate, and so assets are usually balanced by borrowings in that currency.

The exchange risk associated with a foreign denominated instrument is a key element in foreign investment. This risk flows from differential monetary policy and growth in real productivity, which results in differential inflation rates.

   a. Tracking error
   b. Credit risk
   c. Currency risk
   d. Market risk

40. _____ is a financial ratio that indicates the percentage of a company's assets are provided via debt. It is the ratio of total debt (the sum of current liabilities and long-term liabilities) and total assets (the sum of current assets, fixed assets, and other assets such as 'goodwill'.)

>

or alternatively:

>

For example, a company with $2 million in total assets and $500,000 in total liabilities would have a _____ of 25%

Like all financial ratios, a company's _____ should be compared with their industry average or other competing firms.

a. Cash concentration
b. Cash management
c. Capitalization rate
d. Debt ratio

41. In financial accounting, the term _____ is most commonly used to describe any part of shareholders' equity, except for basic share capital. Sometimes, the term is used instead of the term provision; such a use, however, is inconsistent with the terminology suggested by International Accounting Standards Board. For more information about provisions, see provision (accounting.)

a. Treasury stock
b. Reserve
c. Closing entries
d. FIFO and LIFO accounting

42. A _____, reserve bank, or monetary authority is the entity responsible for the monetary policy of a country or of a group of member states. It is a bank that can lend money to other banks in times of need. Its primary responsibility is to maintain the stability of the national currency and money supply, but more active duties include controlling subsidized-loan interest rates, and acting as a lender of last resort to the banking sector during times of financial crisis (private banks often being integral to the national financial system.)

a. Central bank
b. 4-4-5 Calendar
c. 529 plan
d. 7-Eleven

43. A _____ is a payment made by a corporation to its shareholder members. When a corporation earns a profit or surplus, that money can be put to two uses: it can either be re-invested in the business (called retained earnings), or it can be paid to the shareholders as a _____. Many corporations retain a portion of their earnings and pay the remainder as a _____.

a. Dividend yield
b. Dividend puzzle
c. Dividend
d. Special dividend

Chapter 17. Dividend Policy and Internal Financing

1. A _____ is a payment made by a corporation to its shareholder members. When a corporation earns a profit or surplus, that money can be put to two uses: it can either be re-invested in the business (called retained earnings), or it can be paid to the shareholders as a _____. Many corporations retain a portion of their earnings and pay the remainder as a _____.

   a. Dividend
   b. Dividend puzzle
   c. Special dividend
   d. Dividend yield

2. _____ is the fraction of net income a firm pays to its stockholders in dividends:

   The part of the earnings not paid to investors is left for investment to provide for future earnings growth. Investors seeking high current income and limited capital growth prefer companies with high _____. However investors seeking capital growth may prefer lower payout ratio because capital gains are taxed at a lower rate.

   a. Dividend puzzle
   b. Dividend yield
   c. Dividend payout ratio
   d. Dividend imputation

3. _____ is the difference between price and the costs of bringing to market whatever it is that is accounted as an enterprise (whether by harvest, extraction, manufacture, or purchase) in terms of the component costs of delivered goods and/or services and any operating or other expenses.

   A key difficulty in measuring profit is in defining costs. Pure economic monetary profits can be zero or negative even in competitive equilibrium when accounted monetized costs exceed monetized price.

   a. Economic profit
   b. A Random Walk Down Wall Street
   c. AAB
   d. Accounting profit

4. A _____ is a situation that involves losing one quality or aspect of something in return for gaining another quality or aspect. It implies a decision to be made with full comprehension of both the upside and downside of a particular choice.

   In economics the term is expressed as opportunity cost, referring the most preferred alternative given up.

   a. Trade-off
   b. Break-even point
   c. Total revenue
   d. Capital outflow

5. The _____ is the market for securities, where companies and governments can raise longterm funds. The _____ includes the stock market and the bond market. Financial regulators, such as the U.S. Securities and Exchange Commission, oversee the _____s in their designated countries to ensure that investors are protected against fraud.

   a. Forward market
   b. Capital market
   c. Spot rate
   d. Delta neutral

6. A _____ is the price of a single share of a no. of saleable stocks of the company. Once the stock is purchased, the owner becomes a shareholder of the company that issued the share.

Chapter 17. Dividend Policy and Internal Financing

a. Stock split
c. Share price
b. Trading curb
d. Whisper numbers

7. _____ represents the impact on the stock price that investors would cause in reaction to a change in policy of a company.
a. Bonus share
c. Clientele effect
b. Volatility clustering
d. Trade date

8. In economics and contract theory, _____ deals with the study of decisions in transactions where one party has more or better information than the other. This creates an imbalance of power in transactions which can sometimes cause the transactions to go awry. Examples of this problem are adverse selection and moral hazard.
a. ABN Amro
c. A Random Walk Down Wall Street
b. AAB
d. Information asymmetry

9. An _____ is an economic concept that relates to the cost incurred by an entity (such as organizations) associated with problems such as divergent management-shareholder objectives and information asymmetry. The costs consist of two main sources:

1. The costs inherently associated with using an agent (e.g., the risk that agents will use organizational resource for their own benefit) and
2. The costs of techniques used to mitigate the problems associated with using an agent (e.g., the costs of producing financial statements or the use of stock options to align executive interests to shareholder interests.)

Though effects of _____ are present in any agency relationship, the term is most used in business contexts.

The information asymmetry that exists between shareholders and the Chief Executive Officer is generally considered to be a classic example of a principal-agent problem. The agent (the manager) is working on behalf of the principal (the shareholders), who does not observe the actions of the agent.

a. Agency cost
c. A Random Walk Down Wall Street
b. AAB
d. ABN Amro

10. In economics, business, and accounting, a _____ is the value of money that has been used up to produce something, and hence is not available for use anymore. In business, the _____ may be one of acquisition, in which case the amount of money expended to acquire it is counted as _____. In this case, money is the input that is gone in order to acquire the thing.
a. Marginal cost
c. Fixed costs
b. Cost
d. Sliding scale fees

11. _____ is a measure of the ability of a debtor to pay their debts as and when they fall due. It is usually expressed as a ratio or a percentage of current liabilities.

For a corporation with a published balance sheet there are various ratios used to calculate a measure of liquidity.

Chapter 17. Dividend Policy and Internal Financing

a. Operating leverage
c. Operating profit margin
b. Invested capital
d. Accounting liquidity

12. In economics, _____ is a rise in the general level of prices of goods and services in an economy over a period of time. The term '_____' once referred to increases in the money supply (monetary _____); however, economic debates about the relationship between money supply and price levels have led to its primary use today in describing price _____. _____ can also be described as a decline in the real value of money--a loss of purchasing power in the medium of exchange which is also the monetary unit of account.
   a. AAB
   c. ABN Amro
   b. A Random Walk Down Wall Street
   d. Inflation

13. _____ or financing is to provide capital (funds), which means money for a project, a person, a business or any other private or public institutions.

Those funds can be allocated for either short term or long term purposes. The health fund is a new way of _____ private healthcare centers.

   a. Funding
   c. Proxy fight
   b. Product life cycle
   d. Synthetic CDO

14. In business and finance, a _____ (also referred to as equity _____) of stock means a _____ of ownership in a corporation (company.) In the plural, stocks is often used as a synonym for _____s especially in the United States, but it is less commonly used that way outside of North America.

In the United Kingdom, South Africa, and Australia, stock can also refer to completely different financial instruments such as government bonds or, less commonly, to all kinds of marketable securities.

   a. Procter ' Gamble
   c. Share
   b. Bucket shop
   d. Margin

15. _____, refers to consumption opportunity gained by an entity within a specified time frame, which is generally expressed in monetary terms. However, for households and individuals, '_____ is the sum of all the wages, salaries, profits, interests payments, rents and other forms of earnings received... in a given period of time.' For firms, _____ generally refers to net-profit: what remains of revenue after expenses have been subtracted.
   a. OIBDA
   c. Annual report
   b. Accrual
   d. Income

16. An _____ is a tax levied on the financial income of people, corporations, or other legal entities. Various _____ systems exist, with varying degrees of tax incidence. Income taxation can be progressive, proportional, or regressive.
   a. Income tax
   c. AAB
   b. A Random Walk Down Wall Street
   d. ABN Amro

17. In statistics, _____ is used for two things;

- to construct a simple formula that will predict a value or values for a variable given the value of another variable.
- to test whether and how a given variable is related to another variable or variables.

_____ is a form of regression analysis in which the relationship between one or more independent variables and another variable, called the dependent variable, is modelled by a least squares function, called a _____ equation. This function is a linear combination of one or more model parameters, called regression coefficients. A _____ equation with one independent variable represents a straight line when the predicted value (i.e. the dependant variable from the regression equation) is plotted against the independent variable: this is called a simple _____. However, note that 'linear' does not refer to this straight line, but rather to the way in which the regression coefficients occur in the regression equation.

a. Wall Street Crash of 1929
b. Foreign Language and Area Studies
c. Linear regression
d. Stock trader

18. In statistics, _____ refers to techniques for the modeling and analysis of numerical data consisting of values of a dependent variable and of one or more independent variables The dependent variable in the regression equation is modeled as a function of the independent variables, corresponding parameters, and an error term. The error term is treated as a random variable.

a. 529 plan
b. 4-4-5 Calendar
c. Regression analysis
d. 7-Eleven

19. _____ refers to the overarching strategy of the diversified firm. Such a _____ answers the questions of 'in which businesses should we be in?' and 'how does being in these business create synergy and/or add to the competitive advantage of the corporation as a whole?'

Business strategy refers to the aggregated strategies of single business firm or a strategic business unit (SBU) in a diversified corporation. According to Michael Porter, a firm must formulate a business strategy that incorporates either cost leadership, differentiation or focus in order to achieve a sustainable competitive advantage and long-term success in its chosen arenas or industries.

a. 529 plan
b. 7-Eleven
c. 4-4-5 Calendar
d. Corporate strategy

20. The key date to remember for dividend paying stocks is the _____. The _____ is different from the record date. The _____ is typically two trading days before the record date.

In order to receive the upcoming dividend payment payout, you must already own or you must purchase the stock prior to the _____. It is important to note that in most countries, when you buy or sell any stock, there is a three trading-day settlement period on your order.

a. Ex-dividend date
b. Index number
c. Asian Financial Crisis
d. Insolvency

Chapter 17. Dividend Policy and Internal Financing

21. _____ are those dividends paid out in form of additional stock shares of the issuing corporation or other corporation They are usually issued in proportion to shares owned (for example for every 100 shares of stock owned, 5% stock dividend will yield 5 extra shares). If this payment involves the issue of new shares, this is very similar to a stock split in that it increases the total number of shares while lowering the price of each share and does not change the market capitalization or the total value of the shares held
   a. The Hong Kong Securities Institute
   b. Time-based currency
   c. Database auditing
   d. Stock or scrip dividends

22. A _____ or stock divide increases or decreases the number of shares in a public company. The price is adjusted such that the before and after market capitalization of the company remains the same and dilution does not occur. Options and warrants are included.
   a. Stop order
   b. Stop price
   c. Contract for difference
   d. Stock split

23. The institution most often referenced by the word '_____' is a public or publicly traded _____, the shares of which are traded on a public stock exchange (e.g., the New York Stock Exchange or Nasdaq in the United States) where shares of stock of _____s are bought and sold by and to the general public. Most of the largest businesses in the world are publicly traded _____s. However, the majority of _____s are said to be closely held, privately held or close _____s, meaning that no ready market exists for the trading of shares.
   a. Federal Home Loan Mortgage Corporation
   b. Depository Trust Company
   c. Protect
   d. Corporation

24. _____ is a form of corporation equity ownership represented in the securities. It is dangerous in comparison to preferred shares and some other investment options, in that in the event of bankruptcy, _____ investors receive their funds after preferred stockholders, bondholders, creditors, etc. On the other hand, common shares on average perform better than preferred shares or bonds over time.
   a. Stop-limit order
   b. Stock market bubble
   c. Common stock
   d. Stock split

25. In some countries, including the United States and the United Kingdom, corporations can buy back their own stock in a share repurchase, also known as a _____ or share buyback. There has been a meteoric rise in the use of share repurchases in the U.S. in the past twenty years, from $5b in 1980 to $349b in 2005. A share repurchase distributes cash to existing shareholders in exchange for a fraction of the firm's outstanding equity.
   a. Stockholder
   b. Trading curb
   c. Common stock
   d. Stock repurchase

26. _____ in its classic form is defined as a company from one country making a physical investment into building a factory in another country. It is the establishment of an enterprise by a foreigner. Its definition can be extended to include investments made to acquire lasting interest in enterprises operating outside of the economy of the investor.
   a. MicroPlace
   b. Dow Jones ' Company
   c. Foreign direct investment
   d. Public company

Chapter 18. Working-Capital Management and Short-Term Financing

1. _____ are securities that can be easily converted into cash. Such securities will generally have highly liquid markets allowing the security to be sold at a reasonable price very quickly. This is a usual feature in real estate .
   a. Securities lending
   b. Tracking stock
   c. Book entry
   d. Marketable

2. _____ is a financial metric which represents operating liquidity available to a business. Along with fixed assets such as plant and equipment, _____ is considered a part of operating capital. It is calculated as current assets minus current liabilities.
   a. Working capital
   b. 4-4-5 Calendar
   c. 529 plan
   d. Working capital management

3. A _____ is a fungible, negotiable instrument representing financial value. They are broadly categorized into debt securities (such as banknotes, bonds and debentures), and equity securities; e.g., common stocks. The company or other entity issuing the _____ is called the issuer.
   a. Tracking stock
   b. Securities lending
   c. Book entry
   d. Security

4. A _____ is a situation that involves losing one quality or aspect of something in return for gaining another quality or aspect. It implies a decision to be made with full comprehension of both the upside and downside of a particular choice.

   In economics the term is expressed as opportunity cost, referring the most preferred alternative given up.

   a. Break-even point
   b. Capital outflow
   c. Total revenue
   d. Trade-off

5. In accounting, _____ are considered liabilities of the business that are to be settled in cash within the fiscal year or the operating cycle, whichever period is longer.

   For example accounts payable for goods, services or supplies that were purchased for use in the operation of the business and payable within a normal period of time would be _____.

   Bonds, mortgages and loans that are payable over a term exceeding one year would be fixed liabilities.

   a. Closing entries
   b. Gross sales
   c. Net income
   d. Current liabilities

6. In economics, the concept of the _____ refers to the decision-making time frame of a firm in which at least one factor of production is fixed. Costs which are fixed in the _____ have no impact on a firms decisions. For example a firm can raise output by increasing the amount of labour through overtime.
   a. 4-4-5 Calendar
   b. Short-run
   c. 529 plan
   d. Long-run

7. _____ is the provision of resources (such as granting a loan) by one party to another party where that second party does not reimburse the first party immediately, thereby generating a debt, and instead arranges either to repay or return those resources (or material(s) of equal value) at a later date. The first party is called a creditor, also known as a lender, while the second party is called a debtor, also known as a borrower.

Movements of financial capital are normally dependent on either _____ or equity transfers.

a. Credit
b. Clearing house
c. Comparable
d. Warrant

8. _____ is that which is owed; usually referencing assets owed, but the term can cover other obligations. In the case of assets, _____ is a means of using future purchasing power in the present before a summation has been earned. Some companies and corporations use _____ as a part of their overall corporate finance strategy.

a. Partial Payment
b. Cross-collateralization
c. Credit cycle
d. Debt

9. _____ is a life of security. It may also refer to the final payment date of a loan or other financial instrument, at which point all remaining interest and principal is due to be paid.

1, 3, 6 months _____ band can be calculated by using 30-day per month periods.

a. Replacement cost
b. Primary market
c. False billing
d. Maturity

10. _____ is a term applied in many countries to a reference interest rate used by banks. The term originally indicated the rate of interest at which banks lent to favored customers, i.e., those with high credibility, though this is no longer always the case. Some variable interest rates may be expressed as a percentage above or below _____.

a. Time deposit
b. Credit bureau
c. Reserve requirement
d. Prime rate

11. _____ is a fee paid on borrowed assets. It is the price paid for the use of borrowed money, or, money earned by deposited funds. Assets that are sometimes lent with _____ include money, shares, consumer goods through hire purchase, major assets such as aircraft, and even entire factories in finance lease arrangements.

a. A Random Walk Down Wall Street
b. Interest
c. Insolvency
d. AAB

12. _____ is a list for goods and materials held available in stock by a business. It is also used for a list of the contents of a household and for a list for testamentary purposes of the possessions of someone who has died. In accounting _____ is considered an asset.

a. A Random Walk Down Wall Street
b. Inventory
c. ABN Amro
d. AAB

13. _____ exists when one firm provides goods or services to a customer with an agreement to bill them later, or receive a shipment or service from a supplier under an agreement to pay them later. It can be viewed as an essential element of capitalization in an operating business because it can reduce the required capital investment to operate the business if it is managed properly. _____ is the largest use of capital for a majority of business to business (B2B) sellers in the United States and is a critical source of capital for a majority of all businesses.

a. 4-4-5 Calendar
b. Going concern
c. Trade credit
d. 529 plan

Chapter 18. Working-Capital Management and Short-Term Financing

14. In business and accounting, _____s are everything of value that is owned by a person or company. The balance sheet of a firm records the monetary value of the _____s owned by the firm. The two major _____ classes are tangible _____s and intangible _____s.
    a. Income
    b. EBITDA
    c. Accounts payable
    d. Asset

15. _____ or financing is to provide capital (funds), which means money for a project, a person, a business or any other private or public institutions.

    Those funds can be allocated for either short term or long term purposes. The health fund is a new way of _____ private healthcare centers.

    a. Proxy fight
    b. Synthetic CDO
    c. Product life cycle
    d. Funding

16. _____ refers to a business or organization attempting to acquire goods or services to accomplish the goals of the enterprise. Though there are several organizations that attempt to set standards in the _____ process, processes can vary greatly between organizations. Typically the word '_____' is not used interchangeably with the word 'procurement', since procurement typically includes Expediting, Supplier Quality, and Traffic and Logistics (T'L) in addition to _____.
    a. Purchasing
    b. 4-4-5 Calendar
    c. 529 plan
    d. 7-Eleven

17. The _____ measures how long an investment with suppliers deprives a firm of cash -- it is (in the generic case of a retailer) the time between disbursement for inventory and collection on its sale. Thus, the _____ measures how risky it would be to increase this investment with suppliers in the course of expanding customer sales. However, shortening the _____ creates its own risks: while a firm could even achieve a negative _____ by collecting from customers before paying suppliers, a policy of strict collections and lax payments is not always sustainable.
    a. Price/cash flow ratio
    b. Return on capital employed
    c. Return on sales
    d. Cash conversion cycle

18. In accountancy, _____ is a company's average collection period. A low number of days indicates that the company collects its outstanding receivables quickly. Typically, _____ is calculated monthly. The _____ figure is an index of the relationship between outstanding receivables and sales achieved over a given period. The _____ analysis provides general information about the number of days on average that customers take to pay invoices.
    a. Days Sales Outstanding
    b. Round-tripping
    c. Residual value
    d. Net pay

19. The terms _____, nominal _____, and effective _____ describe the interest rate for a whole year (annualized), rather than just a monthly fee/rate, as applied on a loan, mortgage, credit card, etc. Those terms have formal, legal definitions in some countries or legal jurisdictions, but in general:

    - The nominal _____ is the simple-interest rate (for a year.)
    - The effective _____ is the fee+compound interest rate (calculated across a year.)

Chapter 18. Working-Capital Management and Short-Term Financing

The nominal _____ is calculated as: the rate, for a payment period, multiplied by the number of payment periods in a year. However, the exact legal definition of 'effective _____' can vary greatly in each jurisdiction, depending on the type of fees included, such as participation fees, loan origination fees, monthly service charges, or late fees. The effective _____ has been called the 'mathematically-true' interest rate for each year. The computation for the effective _____, as the fee+compound interest rate, can also vary depending on whether the up-front fees, such as origination or participation fees, are added to the entire amount, or treated as a short-term loan due in the first payment.

 a. Annual percentage rate
 b. A Random Walk Down Wall Street
 c. AAB
 d. ABN Amro

20. _____ expresses an annual rate of interest taking into account the effect of compounding, usually for deposit or investment products (such as a certificate of deposit.) It is analogous to the Annual percentage rate (APR), which is used for loans. In some jurisdictions, the use and definition of _____ may be regulated by a government agency, in which case it would generally be capitalized.
 a. Annual percentage yield
 b. A Random Walk Down Wall Street
 c. AAB
 d. ABN Amro

21. In economics, business, and accounting, a _____ is the value of money that has been used up to produce something, and hence is not available for use anymore. In business, the _____ may be one of acquisition, in which case the amount of money expended to acquire it is counted as _____. In this case, money is the input that is gone in order to acquire the thing.
 a. Marginal cost
 b. Sliding scale fees
 c. Fixed costs
 d. Cost

22. In finance, the term _____ describes the amount in cash that returns to the owners of a security. Normally it does not include the price variations, at the difference of the total return. _____ applies to various stated rates of return on stocks (common and preferred, and convertible), fixed income instruments (bonds, notes, bills, strips, zero coupon), and some other investment type insurance products (e.g. annuities.)
 a. Macaulay duration
 b. 4-4-5 Calendar
 c. Yield to maturity
 d. Yield

23. _____, in bookkeeping, refers to assets, liabilities, income, and expenses recorded on individual pages of the so called book of final entry or ledger. Changes in _____ value are made by chronologically posting debit (DR) and credit (CR) entries to its page. Examples of _____s are cash, _____s receivable, mortgages, loans, land and buildings, common stock, sales, services provided, wages, and payroll overhead.
 a. Accretion
 b. Account
 c. Alpha
 d. Option

24. _____ is one of a series of accounting transactions dealing with the billing of customers who owe money to a person, company or organization for goods and services that have been provided to the customer. In most business entities this is typically done by generating an invoice and mailing or electronically delivering it to the customer, who in turn must pay it within an established timeframe called credit or payment terms.

Chapter 18. Working-Capital Management and Short-Term Financing

An example of a common payment term is Net 30, meaning payment is due in the amount of the invoice 30 days from the date of invoice.

   a. Accounts receivable
   b. Accounting methods
   c. Income
   d. Impaired asset

25. _____s are deposits denominated in United States dollars at banks outside the United States, and thus are not under the jurisdiction of the Federal Reserve. Consequently, such deposits are subject to much less regulation than similar deposits within the United States, allowing for higher margins. There is nothing 'European' about _____ deposits; a US dollar-denominated deposit in Tokyo or Caracas would likewise be deemed _____ deposits.
   a. AAB
   b. ABN Amro
   c. A Random Walk Down Wall Street
   d. Eurodollar

26. An _____ is a loan that is not backed by collateral. Also known as a signature loan or personal loan.

_____s are based solely upon the borrower's credit rating.

   a. Annualcreditreport.com
   b. Intelliscore
   c. Event of default
   d. Unsecured loan

27. _____, refers to consumption opportunity gained by an entity within a specified time frame, which is generally expressed in monetary terms. However, for households and individuals, '_____ is the sum of all the wages, salaries, profits, interests payments, rents and other forms of earnings received... in a given period of time.' For firms, _____ generally refers to net-profit: what remains of revenue after expenses have been subtracted.
   a. OIBDA
   b. Annual report
   c. Income
   d. Accrual

28. An _____ is a tax levied on the financial income of people, corporations, or other legal entities. Various _____ systems exist, with varying degrees of tax incidence. Income taxation can be progressive, proportional, or regressive.
   a. ABN Amro
   b. Income tax
   c. AAB
   d. A Random Walk Down Wall Street

29. A '_____' is a 'Charge' that is paid to obtain the right to delay a payment. Essentially, the payer purchases the right to make a given payment in the future instead of in the Present. The '_____', or 'Charge' that must be paid to delay the payment, is simply the difference between what the payment amount would be if it were paid in the present and what the payment amount would be paid if it were paid in the future.
   a. Risk modeling
   b. Risk aversion
   c. Value at risk
   d. Discount

30. A _____ is any credit facility extended to a business by a bank or financial institution. A _____ may take several forms such as cash credit, overdraft, demand loan, export packing credit, term loan, discounting or purchase of commercial bills etc. It is like an account that can readily be tapped into if the need arises or not touched at all and saved for emergencies.

Chapter 18. Worker-Capital Management and Short-Term Financing

a. Line of credit
b. Cash credit
c. Debt-snowball method
d. Default Notice

31. _____ is a type of credit that does not have a fixed number of payments, in contrast to installment credit. Examples of _____s used by consumers include credit cards. Corporate _____ facilities are typically used to provide liquidity for a company's day-to-day operations.
    a. Reverse stock split
    b. Revolving credit
    c. Package loan
    d. Commercial finance

32. A _____ is the maximum amount of credit that a financial institution or other lender will extend to a debtor for a particular line of credit. For example, the maximum that a credit card company will allow a card holder to borrow at any given point on a specific card.

    This limit is based on a variety of factors ranging from an individual's ability to make interest payments, an organization's cashflow and/or ability to repay the principal, to the credit standards employed by the lender.

    a. 7-Eleven
    b. 529 plan
    c. Credit limit
    d. 4-4-5 Calendar

33. In the global money market, _____ is an unsecured promissory note with a fixed maturity of one to 270 days. _____ is a money-market security issued (sold) by large banks and corporations to get money to meet short term debt obligations (for example, payroll), and is only backed by an issuing bank or corporation's promise to pay the face amount on the maturity date specified on the note. Since it is not backed by collateral, only firms with excellent credit ratings from a recognized rating agency will be able to sell their _____ at a reasonable price.
    a. Financial distress
    b. Commercial paper
    c. Trade-off theory
    d. Book building

34. A _____, referred to as a note payable in accounting, is a contract where one party (the maker or issuer) makes an unconditional promise in writing to pay a sum of money to the other (the payee), either at a fixed or determinable future time or on demand of the payee, under specific terms. They differ from IOUs in that they contain a specific promise to pay, rather than simply acknowledging that a debt exists.

    The terms of a note typically include the principal amount, the interest rate if any, and the maturity date.

    a. Title loan
    b. Credit repair software
    c. Promissory note
    d. Financial plan

35. _____ is a financial transaction whereby a business sells its accounts receivable (i.e., invoices) at a discount. _____ differs from a bank loan in three main ways. First, the emphasis is on the value of the receivables (essentially a financial asset), not the firm's credit worthiness.
    a. Credit card balance transfer
    b. Debt-for-equity swap
    c. Financial Literacy Month
    d. Factoring

36. In law, a _____ is a form of security interest granted over an item of property to secure the payment of a debt or performance of some other obligation. The owner of the property, who grants the _____, is referred to as the lienor and the person who has the benefit of the _____ is referred to as the _____ee.

Chapter 18. Working-Capital Management and Short-Term Financing

The etymological root is: Anglo-French _____, loyen bond, restraint, from Latin ligamen, from ligare to bind.

a. Family and Medical Leave Act
c. Joint venture
b. Sarbanes-Oxley Act
d. Lien

37. When companies conduct business across borders, they must deal in foreign currencies. Companies must exchange foreign currencies for home currencies when dealing with receivables, and vice versa for payables. This is done at the current exchange rate between the two countries. _____ is the risk that the exchange rate will change unfavorably before the currency is exchanged.
   a. Foreign exchange risk
   c. Lower of cost or market rule
   b. 529 plan
   d. 4-4-5 Calendar

38. In finance, the _____ between two currencies specifies how much one currency is worth in terms of the other. For example an _____ of 102 Japanese yen to the United States dollar means that JPY 102 is worth the same as USD 1. The foreign exchange market is one of the largest markets in the world.
   a. AAB
   c. ABN Amro
   b. A Random Walk Down Wall Street
   d. Exchange rate

39. _____ is a form of risk that arises from the change in price of one currency against another. Whenever investors or companies have assets or business operations across national borders, they face _____ if their positions are not hedged.

- Transaction risk is the risk that exchange rates will change unfavourably over time. It can be hedged against using forward currency contracts;
- Translation risk is an accounting risk, proportional to the amount of assets held in foreign currencies. Changes in the exchange rate over time will render a report inaccurate, and so assets are usually balanced by borrowings in that currency.

The exchange risk associated with a foreign denominated instrument is a key element in foreign investment. This risk flows from differential monetary policy and growth in real productivity, which results in differential inflation rates.

a. Tracking error
c. Market risk
b. Credit risk
d. Currency risk

Chapter 19. Cash and Marketable Securities Management

1. In United States banking, _____ is a marketing term for certain services offered primarily to larger business customers. It may be used to describe all bank accounts (such as checking accounts) provided to businesses of a certain size, but it is more often used to describe specific services such as cash concentration, zero balance accounting, and automated clearing house facilities. Sometimes, private banking customers are given _____ services.
   - a. Global tactical asset allocation
   - b. Profitability index
   - c. Cash management
   - d. Capitalization rate

2. The _____ is a capital budgeting metric used by firms to decide whether they should make investments. It is an indicator of the efficiency or quality of an investment, as opposed to net present value (NPV), which indicates value or magnitude.

   The IRR is the annualized effective compounded return rate which can be earned on the invested capital, i.e., the yield on the investment.

   - a. AAB
   - b. ABN Amro
   - c. A Random Walk Down Wall Street
   - d. Internal rate of return

3. In business and accounting, _____s are everything of value that is owned by a person or company. The balance sheet of a firm records the monetary value of the _____s owned by the firm. The two major _____ classes are tangible _____s and intangible _____s.
   - a. Accounts payable
   - b. Income
   - c. Asset
   - d. EBITDA

4. In finance, _____, also known as return on investment is the ratio of money gained or lost on an investment relative to the amount of money invested. The amount of money gained or lost may be referred to as interest, profit/loss, gain/loss, or net income/loss. The money invested may be referred to as the asset, capital, principal, or the cost basis of the investment.
   - a. Stock or scrip dividends
   - b. Doctrine of the Proper Law
   - c. Composiition of Creditors
   - d. Rate of return

5. _____ means the inability to pay one's debts as they fall due. Usually used in Business terms, _____ refers to the inability for a 'limited liability' company to pay off debts.

   This is defined in two different ways:

   Cash flow _____ -
       Unable to pay debts as they fall due.
   Balance sheet _____ -
       Having negative net assets: liabilities exceed assets; or net liabilities.

   - a. Interest
   - b. AAB
   - c. A Random Walk Down Wall Street
   - d. Insolvency

6. The _____ is the relationship between the amount of return gained on an investment and the amount of risk undertaken in that investment. The more return sought, the more risk that must be undertaken.

   There are various classes of possible investments, each with their own positions on the overall _____.

Chapter 19. Cash and Marketable Securities Management

a. Blank endorsement
b. Risk-return spectrum
c. Post earnings announcement drift
d. Fiscal sponsorship

7. A _____ is a situation that involves losing one quality or aspect of something in return for gaining another quality or aspect. It implies a decision to be made with full comprehension of both the upside and downside of a particular choice.

In economics the term is expressed as opportunity cost, referring the most preferred alternative given up.

a. Break-even point
b. Trade-off
c. Total revenue
d. Capital outflow

8. The free _____ of a public company is an estimate of the proportion of shares that are not held by large owners and that are not stock with sales restrictions (restricted stock that cannot be sold until they become unrestricted stock.)

The free _____ or a public _____ is usually defined as being all shares held by investors other than:

- shares held by owners owning more than 5% of all shares (those could be institutional investors, 'strategic shareholders,' founders, executives, and other insiders' holdings)
- restricted stocks (granted to executives that can be, but don't have to be, registered insiders)
- insider holdings (it is assumed that insiders hold stock for the very long term)

The free _____ is an important criterion in quoting a share on the stock market.

To _____ a company means to list its shares on a public stock exchange through an initial public offering (or 'flotation'.)

- Open market
- Outstanding shares
- Market capitalization
- Public _____ loat
- Reverse takeover

a. Trade finance
b. Synthetic CDO
c. Float
d. Golden parachute

9. _____, in bookkeeping, refers to assets, liabilities, income, and expenses recorded on individual pages of the so called book of final entry or ledger. Changes in _____ value are made by chronologically posting debit (DR) and credit (CR) entries to its page. Examples of _____s are cash, _____s receivable, mortgages, loans, land and buildings, common stock, sales, services provided, wages, and payroll overhead.

a. Accretion
b. Option
c. Alpha
d. Account

Chapter 19. Cash and Marketable Securities Management   131

10. A _____ can require immediate payment by the second party to the third upon presentation of the _____. This is called a sight _____. A Cheques is a sight _____. An importer might write a _____ promising payment to an exporter for delivery of goods with payment to occur 60 days after the goods are delivered. Such a _____ is called a time _____.

a. Draft
b. Second lien loan
c. Cashflow matching
d. Gross profit margin

11. In economics, business, and accounting, a _____ is the value of money that has been used up to produce something, and hence is not available for use anymore. In business, the _____ may be one of acquisition, in which case the amount of money expended to acquire it is counted as _____. In this case, money is the input that is gone in order to acquire the thing.

a. Cost
b. Fixed costs
c. Marginal cost
d. Sliding scale fees

12. _____ refers to the computer-based systems used to perform financial transactions electronically.

The term is used for a number of different concepts:

- Cardholder-initiated transactions, where a cardholder makes use of a payment card
- Direct deposit payroll payments for a business to its employees, possibly via a payroll services company
- Direct debit payments from customer to business, where the transaction is initiated by the business with customer permission
- Electronic bill payment in online banking, which may be delivered by _____ or paper check
- Transactions involving stored value of electronic money, possibly in a private currency
- Wire transfer via an international banking network (generally carries a higher fee)
- Electronic Benefit Transfer

Electronic funds transferPOS (short for _____ at Point of Sale) is an Australian and New Zealand electronic processing system for credit cards, debit cards and charge cards.

European banks and card companies also sometimes reference 'Electronic funds transferPOS' as the system used for processing card transactions through terminals on points of sale, though the system is not the trademarked Australian/New Zealand variant.

Credit cards

_____ may be initiated by a cardholder when a payment card such as a credit card or debit card is used.

a. A Random Walk Down Wall Street
b. AAB
c. ABN Amro
d. Electronic funds transfer

13. _____ is normally any risk associated with any form of financing.

Depending on the nature of the investment, the type of 'investment' risk will vary. High risk investments have greater potential rewards, but you may lose your money instead by taking the risk for more money.

Chapter 19. Cash and Marketable Securities Management

   a. Liquidating dividend
   c. Revaluation
   b. Stock market index option
   d. Financial risk

14. _____ is a fee paid on borrowed assets. It is the price paid for the use of borrowed money, or, money earned by deposited funds. Assets that are sometimes lent with _____ include money, shares, consumer goods through hire purchase, major assets such as aircraft, and even entire factories in finance lease arrangements.
   a. Insolvency
   c. AAB
   b. A Random Walk Down Wall Street
   d. Interest

15. An _____ is the price a borrower pays for the use of money they do not own, and the return a lender receives for deferring the use of funds, by lending it to the borrower. _____s are normally expressed as a percentage rate over the period of one year.

_____s targets are also a vital tool of monetary policy and are used to control variables like investment, inflation, and unemployment.

   a. Interest rate
   c. A Random Walk Down Wall Street
   b. ABN Amro
   d. AAB

16. _____ is the risk (variability in value) borne by an interest-bearing asset, such as a loan or a bond, due to variability of interest rates. In general, as rates rise, the price of a fixed rate bond will fall, and vice versa. _____ is commonly measured by the bond's duration.
   a. A Random Walk Down Wall Street
   c. International Fisher effect
   b. Interest rate risk
   d. Official bank rate

17. _____ is a list for goods and materials held available in stock by a business. It is also used for a list of the contents of a household and for a list for testamentary purposes of the possessions of someone who has died. In accounting _____ is considered an asset.
   a. ABN Amro
   c. A Random Walk Down Wall Street
   b. AAB
   d. Inventory

18. _____ are securities that can be easily converted into cash. Such securities will generally have highly liquid markets allowing the security to be sold at a reasonable price very quickly. This is a usual feature in real estate.
   a. Book entry
   c. Tracking stock
   b. Marketable
   d. Securities lending

19. A _____ is a fungible, negotiable instrument representing financial value. They are broadly categorized into debt securities (such as banknotes, bonds and debentures), and equity securities; e.g., common stocks. The company or other entity issuing the _____ is called the issuer.
   a. Book entry
   c. Security
   b. Securities lending
   d. Tracking stock

20. _____ is a measure of the ability of a debtor to pay their debts as and when they fall due. It is usually expressed as a ratio or a percentage of current liabilities.

For a corporation with a published balance sheet there are various ratios used to calculate a measure of liquidity.

Chapter 19. Cash and Marketable Securities Management

a. Invested capital
c. Accounting liquidity
b. Operating leverage
d. Operating profit margin

21. _____ mature in one year or less. Like zero-coupon bonds, they do not pay interest prior to maturity; instead they are sold at a discount of the par value to create a positive yield to maturity. Many regard _____ as the least risky investment available to U.S. investors.

a. 4-4-5 Calendar
c. Treasury securities
b. Treasury Inflation Protected Securities
d. Treasury bills

22. In finance, the term _____ describes the amount in cash that returns to the owners of a security. Normally it does not include the price variations, at the difference of the total return. _____ applies to various stated rates of return on stocks (common and preferred, and convertible), fixed income instruments (bonds, notes, bills, strips, zero coupon), and some other investment type insurance products (e.g. annuities.)

a. Macaulay duration
c. 4-4-5 Calendar
b. Yield to maturity
d. Yield

23. _____ is that which is owed; usually referencing assets owed, but the term can cover other obligations. In the case of assets, _____ is a means of using future purchasing power in the present before a summation has been earned. Some companies and corporations use _____ as a part of their overall corporate finance strategy.

a. Partial Payment
c. Debt
b. Credit cycle
d. Cross-collateralization

24. A _____ s a time deposit, a financial product commonly offered to consumers by banks, thrift institutions, and credit unions.

They are similar to savings accounts in that they are insured and thus virtually risk-free; they are 'money in the bank'. They are different from savings accounts in that they have a specific, fixed term (often three months, six months, or one to five years), and, usually, a fixed interest rate.

a. Certificate of deposit
c. Time deposit
b. Variable rate mortgage
d. Reserve requirement

25. In the global money market, _____ is an unsecured promissory note with a fixed maturity of one to 270 days. _____ is a money-market security issued (sold) by large banks and corporations to get money to meet short term debt obligations (for example, payroll), and is only backed by an issuing bank or corporation's promise to pay the face amount on the maturity date specified on the note. Since it is not backed by collateral, only firms with excellent credit ratings from a recognized rating agency will be able to sell their _____ at a reasonable price.

a. Financial distress
c. Book building
b. Trade-off theory
d. Commercial paper

26. A _____ allows a borrower to use a financial security as collateral for a cash loan at a fixed rate of interest. In a repo, the borrower agrees to immediately sell a security to a lender and also agrees to buy the same security from the lender at a fixed price at some later date. A repo is equivalent to a cash transaction combined with a forward contract.

a. Volatility arbitrage
c. Contango
b. Repurchase agreement
d. Total return swap

Chapter 19. Cash and Marketable Securities Management

27. In finance, the _____ is the global financial market for short-term borrowing and lending. It provides short-term liquidity funding for the global financial system. The _____ is where short-term obligations such as Treasury bills, commercial paper and bankers' acceptances are bought and sold.
    a. Cramdown
    b. Debt-for-equity swap
    c. Consumer debt
    d. Money market

28. A _____ is a professionally managed type of collective investment scheme that pools money from many investors and invests it in stocks, bonds, short-term money market instruments, and/or other securities. The _____ will have a fund manager that trades the pooled money on a regular basis. Currently, the worldwide value of all _____ s totals more than $26 trillion.

    Since 1940, there have been three basic types of investment companies in the United States: open-end funds, also known in the US as _____ s; unit investment trusts (UITs); and closed-end funds.

    a. Net asset value
    b. Financial intermediary
    c. Trust company
    d. Mutual fund

29. _____ or financing is to provide capital (funds), which means money for a project, a person, a business or any other private or public institutions.

    Those funds can be allocated for either short term or long term purposes. The health fund is a new way of _____ private healthcare centers.

    a. Proxy fight
    b. Synthetic CDO
    c. Product life cycle
    d. Funding

30. In financial accounting, the term _____ is most commonly used to describe any part of shareholders' equity, except for basic share capital. Sometimes, the term is used instead of the term provision; such a use, however, is inconsistent with the terminology suggested by International Accounting Standards Board. For more information about provisions, see provision (accounting.)
    a. Treasury stock
    b. FIFO and LIFO accounting
    c. Closing entries
    d. Reserve

Chapter 20. Accounts Receivable and Inventory Management

1. _____, in bookkeeping, refers to assets, liabilities, income, and expenses recorded on individual pages of the so called book of final entry or ledger. Changes in _____ value are made by chronologically posting debit (DR) and credit (CR) entries to its page. Examples of _____s are cash, _____s receivable, mortgages, loans, land and buildings, common stock, sales, services provided, wages, and payroll overhead.
   - a. Accretion
   - b. Alpha
   - c. Account
   - d. Option

2. _____ is one of a series of accounting transactions dealing with the billing of customers who owe money to a person, company or organization for goods and services that have been provided to the customer. In most business entities this is typically done by generating an invoice and mailing or electronically delivering it to the customer, who in turn must pay it within an established timeframe called credit or payment terms.

   An example of a common payment term is Net 30, meaning payment is due in the amount of the invoice 30 days from the date of invoice.
   - a. Accounting methods
   - b. Impaired asset
   - c. Income
   - d. Accounts receivable

3. _____ is the provision of resources (such as granting a loan) by one party to another party where that second party does not reimburse the first party immediately, thereby generating a debt, and instead arranges either to repay or return those resources (or material(s) of equal value) at a later date. The first party is called a creditor, also known as a lender, while the second party is called a debtor, also known as a borrower.

   Movements of financial capital are normally dependent on either _____ or equity transfers.
   - a. Clearing house
   - b. Comparable
   - c. Warrant
   - d. Credit

4. _____ and the related Fisher's linear discriminant are methods used in statistics and machine learning to find the linear combination of features which best separate two or more classes of objects or events. The resulting combination may be used as a linear classifier, or, more commonly, for dimensionality reduction before later classification.

   _____ is closely related to ANOVA (analysis of variance) and regression analysis, which also attempt to express one dependent variable as a linear combination of other features or measurements.
   - a. 4-4-5 Calendar
   - b. Linear discriminant analysis
   - c. 529 plan
   - d. 7-Eleven

5. _____ is one of the accounting liquidity ratios, a financial ratio. This ratio measures the number of times, on average, receivables (e.g. Accounts Receivable) are collected during the period. A popular variant of the _____ is to convert it into an Average Collection Period in terms of days.
   - a. Sharpe ratio
   - b. PEG ratio
   - c. Return on equity
   - d. Receivables turnover ratio

Chapter 20. Accounts Receivable and Inventory Management

6. In finance, the term _____ describes the amount in cash that returns to the owners of a security. Normally it does not include the price variations, at the difference of the total return. _____ applies to various stated rates of return on stocks (common and preferred, and convertible), fixed income instruments (bonds, notes, bills, strips, zero coupon), and some other investment type insurance products (e.g. annuities.)
   a. Yield
   b. Macaulay duration
   c. Yield to maturity
   d. 4-4-5 Calendar

7. The _____ or redemption yield is the yield promised to the bondholder on the assumption that the bond or other fixed-interest security such as gilts will be held to maturity, that all coupon and principal payments will be made and coupon payments are reinvested at the bond's promised yield at the same rate as invested. It is a measure of the return of the bond. This technique in theory allows investors to calculate the fair value of different financial instruments.
   a. 4-4-5 Calendar
   b. Yield to maturity
   c. Yield
   d. Macaulay duration

8. _____ is a life of security. It may also refer to the final payment date of a loan or other financial instrument, at which point all remaining interest and principal is due to be paid.

   1, 3, 6 months _____ band can be calculated by using 30-day per month periods.

   a. Primary market
   b. Replacement cost
   c. False billing
   d. Maturity

9. _____ is a list for goods and materials held available in stock by a business. It is also used for a list of the contents of a household and for a list for testamentary purposes of the possessions of someone who has died. In accounting _____ is considered an asset.
   a. Inventory
   b. ABN Amro
   c. AAB
   d. A Random Walk Down Wall Street

10. In finance, a _____ or accounting ratio is a ratio of two selected numerical values taken from an enterprise's financial statements. There are many standard ratios used to try to evaluate the overall financial condition of a corporation or other organization. They may be used by managers within a firm, by current and potential shareholders (owners) of a firm, and by a firm's creditors. Security analysts use these to compare the strengths and weaknesses in various companies.
    a. Sustainable growth rate
    b. Price/cash flow ratio
    c. Financial ratio
    d. Return on capital employed

11. _____ is a term used by inventory specialists to describe a level of extra stock that is maintained below the cycle stock to buffer against stockouts. _____ exists to counter uncertainties in supply and demand. _____ is defined as extra units of inventory carried as protection against possible stockouts .(shortfall in raw material or packaging.)
    a. Counting house
    b. Golden parachute
    c. Funding
    d. Safety stock

12. _____ is an inventory strategy implemented to improve the return on investment of a business by reducing in-process inventory and its associated carrying costs. In order to achieve _____ the process must have signals of what is going on elsewhere within the process. This means that the process is often driven by a series of signals, which can be Kanban, that tell production processes when to make the next part.

a. Greed and fear
c. Debtor-in-possession financing
b. Just-in-time
d. Pac-Man defense

13. In economics, business, and accounting, a _____ is the value of money that has been used up to produce something, and hence is not available for use anymore. In business, the _____ may be one of acquisition, in which case the amount of money expended to acquire it is counted as _____. In this case, money is the input that is gone in order to acquire the thing.
   a. Cost
   c. Marginal cost
   b. Fixed costs
   d. Sliding scale fees

14. _____ is the discipline of identifying, monitoring and limiting risks. In some cases the acceptable risk may be near zero. Risks can come from accidents, natural causes and disasters as well as deliberate attacks from an adversary.
   a. Penny stock
   c. Risk management
   b. FIFO
   d. 4-4-5 Calendar

Chapter 21. Risk Management

1. A _____ is a financial contract whose value is derived from the value of something else (known as the underlying.) The underlying on which a _____ is based can be an asset, weather conditions bonds or other forms of credit.
    a. 529 plan
    b. 7-Eleven
    c. 4-4-5 Calendar
    d. Derivative

2. In finance, a _____ is a standardized contract, to buy or sell a specified commodity of standardized quality at a certain date in the future, at a market determined price (the futures price.)

    The price is determined by the instantaneous equilibrium between the forces of supply and demand among competing buy and sell orders on the exchange at the time of the purchase or sale of the contract.

    In many cases, the items may be such non-traditional 'commodities' as foreign currencies, commercial or government paper [e.g., bonds], or 'baskets' of corporate equity ['stock indices'] or other financial instruments.

    a. Repurchase agreement
    b. Heston model
    c. Futures contract
    d. Financial future

3. _____ is the discipline of identifying, monitoring and limiting risks. In some cases the acceptable risk may be near zero. Risks can come from accidents, natural causes and disasters as well as deliberate attacks from an adversary.
    a. 4-4-5 Calendar
    b. Penny stock
    c. Risk management
    d. FIFO

4. A _____ is an exchange of promises between two or more parties to do an act which is enforceable in a court of law. It is where an unqualified offer meets a qualified acceptance and the parties reach Consensus ad Idem. The parties must have the necessary capacity to _____ and the _____ must not be either trifling, indeterminate, impossible or illegal.
    a. 529 plan
    b. Contract
    c. 7-Eleven
    d. 4-4-5 Calendar

5. A _____ is a financial services company that provides clearing and settlement services for financial transactions, usually on a futures exchange, and often acts as central counterparty (the payor actually pays the _____, which then pays the payee). A _____ may also offer novation, the substitution of a new contract or debt for an old, or other credit enhancement services to its members.

    The term is also used for banks like Suffolk Bank that acted as a restraint on the over-issuance of private bank notes.

    a. Warrant
    b. Clearing house
    c. Valuation
    d. Bucket shop

6. The _____ requirement is the amount required to be collateralized in order to open a position. Thereafter, the amount required to be kept in collateral until the position is closed is the maintenance requirement. The maintenance requirement is the minimum amount to be collateralized in order to keep an open position.
    a. Arbitrage
    b. Issuer
    c. Efficient-market hypothesis
    d. Initial margin

Chapter 21. Risk Management

7. The _____ is the amount required to be collateralized in order to open a position. Thereafter, the amount required to be kept in collateral until the position is closed is the maintenance requirement. The maintenance requirement is the minimum amount to be collateralized in order to keep an open position.
    a. ABN Amro
    b. A Random Walk Down Wall Street
    c. Initial margin requirement
    d. AAB

8. The variation margin or _____ is not collateral, but a daily offsetting of profits and losses. Futures are marked-to-market every day, so the current price is compared to the previous day's price. The profit or loss on the day of a position is then paid to or debited from the holder by the futures exchange.
    a. Maintenance margin
    b. Total return swap
    c. Delivery month
    d. SPI 200 futures contract

9. In finance, a _____ is collateral that the holder of a position in securities, options, or futures contracts has to deposit to cover the credit risk of his counterparty (most often his broker.) This risk can arise if the holder has done any of the following:

    - borrowed cash from the counterparty to buy securities or options,
    - sold securities or options short, or
    - entered into a futures contract.

The collateral can be in the form of cash or securities, and it is deposited in a _____ account. On U.S. futures exchanges, '_____' was formally called performance bond.

_____ buying is buying securities with cash borrowed from a broker, using other securities as collateral.

    a. Procter ' Gamble
    b. Credit
    c. Share
    d. Margin

10. A _____ is something for which there is demand, but which is supplied without qualitative differentiation across a market. It is a product that is the same no matter who produces it, such as petroleum, notebook paper, or milk. In other words, copper is copper.
    a. 529 plan
    b. 7-Eleven
    c. 4-4-5 Calendar
    d. Commodity

11. A _____ is a futures contract on a short term interest rate (STIR.) Contracts vary, but are often defined on an interest rate index such as 3-month sterling or US dollar LIBOR.

They are traded across a wide range of currencies, including the G12 country currencies and many others.

    a. Dual currency deposit
    b. Notional amount
    c. Real estate derivatives
    d. Financial future

12. _____ is a fee paid on borrowed assets. It is the price paid for the use of borrowed money, or, money earned by deposited funds. Assets that are sometimes lent with _____ include money, shares, consumer goods through hire purchase, major assets such as aircraft, and even entire factories in finance lease arrangements.

a. A Random Walk Down Wall Street
b. AAB
c. Insolvency
d. Interest

13. An _____ is the price a borrower pays for the use of money they do not own, and the return a lender receives for deferring the use of funds, by lending it to the borrower. _____s are normally expressed as a percentage rate over the period of one year.

_____s targets are also a vital tool of monetary policy and are used to control variables like investment, inflation, and unemployment.

a. AAB
b. ABN Amro
c. A Random Walk Down Wall Street
d. Interest rate

14. An _____ is a futures contract with an interest-bearing instrument as the underlying asset.

Examples include Treasury-bill futures, Treasury-bond futures and Eurodollar futures.

The global market for exchange-traded _____s is notionally valued by the Bank for International Settlements at $5,794,200 million in 2005.

a. Equity swap
b. Interest rate derivative
c. Open interest
d. Interest rate future

15. _____ is the planning process used to determine whether a firm's long term investments such as new machinery, replacement machinery, new plants, new products, and research development projects are worth pursuing. It is budget for major capital, or investment, expenditures.

Many formal methods are used in _____, including the techniques such as

- Net present value
- Profitability index
- Internal rate of return
- Modified Internal Rate of Return
- Equivalent annuity

These methods use the incremental cash flows from each potential investment, or project. Techniques based on accounting earnings and accounting rules are sometimes used - though economists consider this to be improper - such as the accounting rate of return, and 'return on investment.' Simplified and hybrid methods are used as well, such as payback period and discounted payback period.

a. Financial distress
b. Shareholder value
c. Preferred stock
d. Capital budgeting

16. A _____ is a point at which a stock market will stop trading for a period of time in response to substantial drops in value.

Chapter 21. Risk Management 141

On the New York Stock Exchange, one type of _____ is referred to as a 'circuit breaker.' These limits were put in place after Black Monday in order to reduce market volatility and massive panic sell-offs, giving traders time to reconsider their transactions.

At the start of each quarter, the NYSE sets three circuit breaker levels at levels of 10%, 20%, and 30% of the average closing price of the Dow Jones Industrial Average for the month preceding the start of the quarter, rounded to the nearest 50-point interval.

   a. Trading curb
   c. Stock market index
   b. Stock repurchase
   d. Common stock

17. The _____ is one of several stock market indices, created by nineteenth-century Wall Street Journal editor and Dow Jones ' Company co-founder Charles Dow. Dow compiled the index to gauge the performance of the industrial sector of the American stock market. It is the second-oldest U.S. market index, after the Dow Jones Transportation Average, which Dow also created.
   a. 529 plan
   c. 4-4-5 Calendar
   b. 7-Eleven
   d. Dow Jones Industrial Average

18. A _____ is a method of measuring a section of the stock market. Many indices are cited by news or financial services firms and are used to benchmark the performance of portfolios such as mutual funds.
   a. Stop order
   c. Trading curb
   b. Program trading
   d. Stock market index

19. An _____ is a contract written by a seller that conveys to the buyer the right -- but not the obligation -- to buy (in the case of a call _____) or to sell (in the case of a put _____) a particular asset, such as a piece of property such as, among others, a futures contract. In return for granting the _____, the seller collects a payment (the premium) from the buyer.

For example, buying a call _____ provides the right to buy a specified quantity of a security at a set strike price at some time on or before expiration, while buying a put _____ provides the right to sell.

   a. Amortization
   c. Option
   b. Annuity
   d. AT'T Mobility LLC

20. A _____ is a financial contract between two parties, the buyer and the seller of this type of option. Often it is simply labeled a 'call'. The buyer of the option has the right, but not the obligation to buy an agreed quantity of a particular commodity or financial instrument (the underlying instrument) from the seller of the option at a certain time (the expiration date) for a certain price (the strike price.)
   a. Bull spread
   c. Bear call spread
   b. Bear spread
   d. Call option

21. In options, the _____ is a key variable in a derivatives contract between two parties. Where the contract requires delivery of the underlying instrument, the trade will be at the _____, regardless of the spot price (market price) of the underlying instrument at that time.

Chapter 21. Risk Management

Definition - The fixed price at which the owner of an option can purchase, in the case of a call in the case of a put, the underlying security or commodity.

a. Naked put
c. Moneyness
b. Strike price
d. Swaption

22. A _____ is a financial contract between two parties, the seller (writer) and the buyer of the option. The put allows its buyer the right but not the obligation to sell a commodity or financial instrument (the underlying instrument) to the writer (seller) of the option at a certain time for a certain price (the strike price.) The writer (seller) has the obligation to purchase the underlying asset at that strike price, if the buyer exercises the option.

a. Bear spread
c. Bear call spread
b. Put option
d. Debit spread

23. In finance, a _____ in a security, such as a stock or a bond means the holder of the position owns the security and will profit if the price of the security goes up.

Similarly, a _____ in a futures contract or similar derivative, means the holder of the position will profit if the price of the underlying security goes up. Going long is the more conventional practice of investing and is contrasted with going short

- Short (finance)

a. Central Securities Depository
c. Delta hedging
b. Long position
d. Forward market

24. Days to Cover (DTC) is a numerical term that describes the relationship between the amount of shares in a given equity that have been short sold and the number of days of typical trading that it would require to 'cover' all _____ outstanding. For example, if there are ten million shares of XYZ Inc. that are currently short sold and the average daily volume of XYZ shares traded each day is one million, it would require ten days of trading for all _____ to be covered (10 million / 1 million.)

a. Stock or scrip dividends
c. Guaranteed investment contracts
b. Short positions
d. Cash budget

25. A _____ is a transaction in which the seller of call options already owns the corresponding amount of the underlying instrument, such as shares of a stock or other securities. These owned shares provide the 'cover' as they can be handed over to the buyer of the options when he decides to exercise them, instead of having to buy the optioned shares at unfavorable market prices in the case of 'uncovered' or short call. Thus, the _____ limits the (potentially unlimited) loss that results from a short call when the price of the underlying stock moves above the strike price of the option.

a. 529 plan
c. 4-4-5 Calendar
b. 7-Eleven
d. Covered call

26. In finance, _____ refers to the value of a security which is intrinsic to or contained in the security itself. It is also frequently called fundamental value. It is ordinarily calculated by summing the future income generated by the asset, and discounting it to the present value.

Chapter 21. Risk Management

a. Amortization
b. Alpha
c. Accretion
d. Intrinsic value

27. A _____ occurs when a speculator writes (sells) a call option on a security without ownership of that security. It is one of the riskiest options strategies because it carries unlimited risk as opposed to a naked put where the maximum loss occurs if the stock falls to zero.

The buyer of a call option has the right to buy a specific number of shares at a strike price before an expiration date from the call option seller.

a. Rate of return
b. Bed Bath ' Beyond Inc.
c. Comanity
d. Naked call

28. _____ denotes the total number of derivative contracts, like futures and options, that are currently active on a specific underlying security, having specific terms.

Namely, the total contracts for a specific strike price and expiration date, that have been traded, but have not yet expired, have not yet been closed through a closing transaction, or have not yet been terminated via early exercise. A closing transaction occurs when a counterparty that longs the contract sells, or, conversely, when a counterparty that shorts the contract buys.

a. Equity derivative
b. Equity swap
c. International Swaps and Derivatives Association
d. Open interest

29. The _____ is the price the buyer of the options contract pays for the right to buy or sell a security at a specified price in the future.

a. A Random Walk Down Wall Street
b. ABN Amro
c. AAB
d. Option premium

30. An _____ option has no intrinsic value. A call option is _____ when the strike price is above the spot price of the underlying security. A put option is _____ when the strike price is below the spot price.

a. AAB
b. Out-of-the-money
c. A Random Walk Down Wall Street
d. ABN Amro

31. In finance, the value of an option consists of two components, its intrinsic value and its _____. Time value is simply the difference between option value and intrinsic value. _____ is also known as theta, extrinsic value, or instrumental value.

a. Global Squeeze
b. Conservatism
c. Time value
d. Debt buyer

32. In finance, _____ (or gearing) is borrowing money to supplement existing funds for investment in such a way that the potential positive or negative outcome is magnified and/or enhanced. It generally refers to using borrowed funds, or debt, so as to attempt to increase the returns to equity. Deleveraging is the action of reducing borrowings.

a. Financial endowment
b. Leverage
c. Pension fund
d. Limited partnership

Chapter 21. Risk Management

33. In banking and finance, _____ denotes all activities from the time a commitment is made for a transaction until it is settled. _____ is necessary because the speed of trades is much faster than the cycle time for completing the underlying transaction.

In its widest sense _____ involves the management of post-trading, pre-settlement credit exposures, to ensure that trades are settled in accordance with market rules, even if a buyer or seller should become insolvent prior to settlement.

   a. Procter ' Gamble
   b. Clearing
   c. Clearing house
   d. Share

34. The institution most often referenced by the word '_____' is a public or publicly traded _____, the shares of which are traded on a public stock exchange (e.g., the New York Stock Exchange or Nasdaq in the United States) where shares of stock of _____s are bought and sold by and to the general public. Most of the largest businesses in the world are publicly traded _____s. However, the majority of _____s are said to be closely held, privately held or close _____s, meaning that no ready market exists for the trading of shares.

   a. Corporation
   b. Federal Home Loan Mortgage Corporation
   c. Depository Trust Company
   d. Protect

35. _____ is a derivative financial instrument.

The global market for exchange-traded _____s is notionally valued by the Bank for International Settlements at $3,075,400 million in 2005.

   a. Interest rate option
   b. Economic entity
   c. Education production function
   d. Eurobond

36. _____ are government bonds issued by the United States Department of the Treasury through the Bureau of the Public Debt. They are the debt financing instruments of the U.S. Federal government, and they are often referred to simply as Treasuries or Treasurys. There are four types of marketable _____: Treasury bills, Treasury notes, Treasury bonds, and Treasury Inflation Protected Securities (TIPS.)

   a. Treasury Inflation-Protected Securities
   b. 4-4-5 Calendar
   c. Treasury Inflation Protected Securities
   d. Treasury securities

37. In finance, a _____ is a debt security, in which the authorized issuer owes the holders a debt and, depending on the terms of the _____, is obliged to pay interest (the coupon) and/or to repay the principal at a later date, termed maturity.

Thus a _____ is a loan: the issuer is the borrower, the _____ holder is the lender, and the coupon is the interest. _____s provide the borrower with external funds to finance long-term investments, or, in the case of government _____s, to finance current expenditure.

   a. Convertible bond
   b. Puttable bond
   c. Bond
   d. Catastrophe bonds

Chapter 21. Risk Management

38. A _____ is a foreign exchange agreement between two parties to exchange principal and fixed rate interest payments on a loan in one currency for principal and fixed rate interest payments on an equal (regarding net present value) loan in another currency. They are motivated by comparative advantage.
   a. Forex swap
   b. Currency swap
   c. Currency pair
   d. Foreign exchange market

39. In economic models, the _____ time frame assumes no fixed factors of production. Firms can enter or leave the marketplace, and the cost (and availability) of land, labor, raw materials, and capital goods can be assumed to vary. In contrast, in the short-run time frame, certain factors are assumed to be fixed, because there is not sufficient time for them to change.
   a. 4-4-5 Calendar
   b. Short-run
   c. 529 plan
   d. Long-run

40. A _____ is a fungible, negotiable instrument representing financial value. They are broadly categorized into debt securities (such as banknotes, bonds and debentures), and equity securities; e.g., common stocks. The company or other entity issuing the _____ is called the issuer.
   a. Tracking stock
   b. Securities lending
   c. Book entry
   d. Security

41. In finance, a _____ is a derivative in which two counterparties agree to exchange one stream of cash flows against another stream. These streams are called the legs of the _____.

The cash flows are calculated over a notional principal amount, which is usually not exchanged between counterparties.

   a. Volatility swap
   b. Local volatility
   c. Swap
   d. Volatility arbitrage

42. _____ or financing is to provide capital (funds), which means money for a project, a person, a business or any other private or public institutions.

Those funds can be allocated for either short term or long term purposes. The health fund is a new way of _____ private healthcare centers.

   a. Synthetic CDO
   b. Proxy fight
   c. Product life cycle
   d. Funding

43. In finance, a _____ is a type of bond that can be converted into shares of stock in the issuing company, usually at some pre-announced ratio. It is a hybrid security with debt- and equity-like features. Although it typically has a low coupon rate, the holder is compensated with the ability to convert the bond to common stock, usually at a substantial discount to the stock's market value.
   a. Convertible bond
   b. Bond fund
   c. Corporate bond
   d. Gilts

Chapter 21. Risk Management

44. In finance, _____ is the process of estimating the potential market value of a financial asset or liability. they can be done on assets (for example, investments in marketable securities such as stocks, options, business enterprises, or intangible assets such as patents and trademarks) or on liabilities (e.g., Bonds issued by a company.) _____s are required in many contexts including investment analysis, capital budgeting, merger and acquisition transactions, financial reporting, taxable events to determine the proper tax liability, and in litigation.
    a. Share
    b. Valuation
    c. Margin
    d. Procter ' Gamble

45. In finance, a _____ is a security that entitles the holder to buy stock of the company that issued it at a specified price, which is usually higher than the stock price at time of issue.

    _____s are frequently attached to bonds or preferred stock as a sweetener, allowing the issuer to pay lower interest rates or dividends. They can be used to enhance the yield of the bond, and make them more attractive to potential buyers.

    a. Clearing house
    b. Clearing
    c. Credit
    d. Warrant

46. In economics and finance, _____ is the practice of taking advantage of a price differential between two or more markets: striking a combination of matching deals that capitalize upon the imbalance, the profit being the difference between the market prices. When used by academics, an _____ is a transaction that involves no negative cash flow at any probabilistic or temporal state and a positive cash flow in at least one state; in simple terms, a risk-free profit.
    a. Initial margin
    b. Efficient-market hypothesis
    c. Issuer
    d. Arbitrage

Chapter 22. International Business Finance

1. _____ or financing is to provide capital (funds), which means money for a project, a person, a business or any other private or public institutions.

Those funds can be allocated for either short term or long term purposes. The health fund is a new way of _____ private healthcare centers.

   a. Synthetic CDO
   c. Product life cycle
   b. Proxy fight
   d. Funding

2. In economics, the _____, measures the payments that flow between any individual country and all other countries. It is used to summarize all international economic transactions for that country during a specific time period, usually a year. The _____ is determined by the country's exports and imports of goods, services, and financial capital, as well as financial transfers.

   a. Balance of payments
   c. Gross national product
   b. Purchasing power parity
   d. 4-4-5 Calendar

3. _____ is a reduction in the value of a currency with respect to other monetary units. In common modern usage, it specifically implies an official lowering of the value of a country's currency within a fixed exchange rate system, by which the monetary authority formally sets a new fixed rate with respect to a foreign reference currency. In contrast, (currency) depreciation is used for the unofficial decrease in the exchange rate in a floating exchange rate system.

   a. Reserve currency
   c. Currency board
   b. Devaluation
   d. Petrodollar recycling

4. _____ means a rise of a price of goods or products. This term is specially used as _____ of a currency, where it means a rise of currency to the relation with a foreign currency in a fixed exchange rate. In floating exchange rate correct term would be appreciation.

   a. Correlation trading
   c. Common pool problem
   b. Holding period return
   d. Revaluation

5. In finance, the _____ between two currencies specifies how much one currency is worth in terms of the other. For example an _____ of 102 Japanese yen to the United States dollar means that JPY 102 is worth the same as USD 1. The foreign exchange market is one of the largest markets in the world.

   a. ABN Amro
   c. A Random Walk Down Wall Street
   b. Exchange rate
   d. AAB

6. The _____ is where currency trading takes place. It is where banks and other official institutions facilitate the buying and selling of foreign currencies. FX transactions typically involve one party purchasing a quantity of one currency in exchange for paying a quantity of another.

   a. Spot market
   c. Foreign exchange option
   b. Foreign exchange market
   d. Floating exchange rate

7. The _____ or spot rate of a commodity, a security or a currency is the price that is quoted for immediate (spot) settlement (payment and delivery.) Spot settlement is normally one or two business days from trade date. This is in contrast with the forward price established in a forward contract or futures contract, where contract terms (price) are set now, but delivery and payment will occur at a future date.

a. Cost of carry
b. Market price
c. Central Securities Depository
d. Spot price

8. In economics and finance, _____ is the practice of taking advantage of a price differential between two or more markets: striking a combination of matching deals that capitalize upon the imbalance, the profit being the difference between the market prices. When used by academics, an _____ is a transaction that involves no negative cash flow at any probabilistic or temporal state and a positive cash flow in at least one state; in simple terms, a risk-free profit.

a. Efficient-market hypothesis
b. Initial margin
c. Issuer
d. Arbitrage

9. _____ are a currency pair that does not include USD, such as GBP/JPY. Pairs that involve the EUR are called euro crosses, such as EUR/GBP. All other currency pairs (those that don't involve USD or EUR) are generally referred to as _____.

a. Foreign exchange risk
b. 529 plan
c. 4-4-5 Calendar
d. Cross rates

10. _____ refers to taking advantage of a state of imbalance between three foreign exchange markets: a combination of matching deals are struck that exploit the imbalance, the profit being the difference between the market prices.

_____ offers a risk-free profit (in theory), so opportunities for _____ usually disappear quickly, as many people are looking for them, or simply never occur as everybody knows the pricing relation.

Consider the three foreign exchange rates among the Canadian dollar, the U.S. dollar, and the Australian dollar.

a. Floating exchange rate
b. Currency future
c. Currency pair
d. Triangular arbitrage

11. _____ is a form of risk that arises from the change in price of one currency against another. Whenever investors or companies have assets or business operations across national borders, they face _____ if their positions are not hedged.

- Transaction risk is the risk that exchange rates will change unfavourably over time. It can be hedged against using forward currency contracts;
- Translation risk is an accounting risk, proportional to the amount of assets held in foreign currencies. Changes in the exchange rate over time will render a report inaccurate, and so assets are usually balanced by borrowings in that currency.

The exchange risk associated with a foreign denominated instrument is a key element in foreign investment. This risk flows from differential monetary policy and growth in real productivity, which results in differential inflation rates.

a. Market risk
b. Currency risk
c. Credit risk
d. Tracking error

12. A _____ is an exchange of promises between two or more parties to do an act which is enforceable in a court of law. It is where an unqualified offer meets a qualified acceptance and the parties reach Consensus ad Idem. The parties must have the necessary capacity to _____ and the _____ must not be either trifling, indeterminate, impossible or illegal.
   a. 7-Eleven
   b. 529 plan
   c. 4-4-5 Calendar
   d. Contract

13. A '_____' is a 'Charge' that is paid to obtain the right to delay a payment. Essentially, the payer purchases the right to make a given payment in the future instead of in the Present. The '_____', or 'Charge' that must be paid to delay the payment, is simply the difference between what the payment amount would be if it were paid in the present and what the payment amount would be paid if it were paid in the future.
   a. Risk aversion
   b. Discount
   c. Risk modeling
   d. Value at risk

14. In economics and finance, _____ represents passive holdings of securities such as foreign stocks, bonds, or other financial assets, none of which entails active management or control of the securities' issuer by the investor; where such control exists, it is known as foreign direct investment. Generally, this means the investor holds less than 10% of the total shares or less than the amount needed to hold the majority vote.

Some examples of _____ are:

- purchase of shares in a foreign company.
- purchase of bonds issued by a foreign government.
- acquisition of assets in a foreign country.

Factors affecting international _____:

- tax rates on interest or dividends (investors will normally prefer countries where the tax rates are relatively low)
- interest rates (money tends to flow to countries with high interest rates)
- exchange rates (foreign investors may be attracted if the local currency is expected to strengthen)

_____ is part of the capital account on the balance of payments statistics.

   a. Divestment
   b. Portable alpha
   c. Tactical asset allocation
   d. Portfolio investment

15. _____ is a fee paid on borrowed assets. It is the price paid for the use of borrowed money, or, money earned by deposited funds. Assets that are sometimes lent with _____ include money, shares, consumer goods through hire purchase, major assets such as aircraft, and even entire factories in finance lease arrangements.
   a. A Random Walk Down Wall Street
   b. Insolvency
   c. AAB
   d. Interest

16. An _____ is the price a borrower pays for the use of money they do not own, and the return a lender receives for deferring the use of funds, by lending it to the borrower. _____s are normally expressed as a percentage rate over the period of one year.

_____s targets are also a vital tool of monetary policy and are used to control variables like investment, inflation, and unemployment.

a. ABN Amro
b. A Random Walk Down Wall Street
c. AAB
d. Interest rate

17. _____ is an economic concept, expressed as a basic algebraic identity that relates interest rates and exchange rates. The identity is theoretical, and usually follows from assumptions imposed in economics models. There is evidence to support as well as to refute the concept.

a. Unit price
b. AAB
c. A Random Walk Down Wall Street
d. Interest rate parity

18. In economics, the _____ is the proposition by Irving Fisher that the real interest rate is independent of monetary measures, especially the nominal interest rate. The Fisher equation is

$$r_r = r_n >- >\pi^e.$$

This means, the real interest rate (r_r) equals the nominal interest rate (r_n) minus expected rate of inflation ($>\pi^e$.) Here all the rates are continuously compounded.

a. Fisher hypothesis
b. 7-Eleven
c. 529 plan
d. 4-4-5 Calendar

19. The _____ is an economic law stated as: 'In an efficient market all identical goods must have only one price.'

The intuition for this law is that all sellers will flock to the highest prevailing price, and all buyers to the lowest current market price. In an efficient market the convergence on one price is instant.

Commodities can be traded on financial markets, where there will be a single offer price, and bid price.

a. Liability
b. Letter of credit
c. Law of one price
d. Personal property

20. The _____ is a hypothesis in international finance that says that the difference in the nominal interest rates between two countries determines the movement of the nominal exchange rate between their currencies, with the value of the currency of the country with the lower nominal interest rate increasing. This is also known as the assumption of Uncovered Interest Parity.

The Fisher hypothesis says that the real interest rate in an economy is independent of monetary variables.

a. International Fisher effect
b. A Random Walk Down Wall Street
c. Official bank rate
d. Interest rate risk

Chapter 22. International Business Finance

21. In finance, a _____ is a position established in one market in an attempt to offset exposure to the price risk of an equal but opposite obligation or position in another market -- usually, but not always, in the context of one's commercial activity. Hedging is a strategy designed to minimize exposure to such business risks as a sharp contraction in demand for one's inventory, while still allowing the business to profit from producing and maintaining that inventory. A typical hedger might be a farmer with 2000 acres of unharvested wheat in the ground, who would rather tend his crop without the distraction of uncertain prices.
   a. 4-4-5 Calendar
   c. 7-Eleven
   b. 529 plan
   d. Hedge

22. A _____, also FX future or foreign exchange future, is a futures contract to exchange one currency for another at a specified date in the future at a price (exchange rate) that is fixed on the purchase date. Typically, one of the currencies is the US dollar. The price of a future is then in terms of US dollars per unit of other currency.
   a. Currency swap
   c. Foreign exchange controls
   b. Currency future
   d. Non-deliverable forward

23. In finance, a _____ is a standardized contract, to buy or sell a specified commodity of standardized quality at a certain date in the future, at a market determined price (the futures price.)

The price is determined by the instantaneous equilibrium between the forces of supply and demand among competing buy and sell orders on the exchange at the time of the purchase or sale of the contract.

In many cases, the items may be such non-traditional 'commodities' as foreign currencies, commercial or government paper [e.g., bonds], or 'baskets' of corporate equity ['stock indices'] or other financial instruments.

   a. Financial future
   c. Heston model
   b. Futures contract
   d. Repurchase agreement

24. An _____ is a contract written by a seller that conveys to the buyer the right -- but not the obligation -- to buy (in the case of a call _____) or to sell (in the case of a put _____) a particular asset, such as a piece of property such as, among others, a futures contract. In return for granting the _____, the seller collects a payment (the premium) from the buyer.

For example, buying a call _____ provides the right to buy a specified quantity of a security at a set strike price at some time on or before expiration, while buying a put _____ provides the right to sell.

   a. Amortization
   c. AT'T Mobility LLC
   b. Option
   d. Annuity

25. _____ are securities that can be easily converted into cash. Such securities will generally have highly liquid markets allowing the security to be sold at a reasonable price very quickly. This is a usual feature in real estate .
   a. Marketable
   c. Tracking stock
   b. Securities lending
   d. Book entry

26. A _____ is a fungible, negotiable instrument representing financial value. They are broadly categorized into debt securities (such as banknotes, bonds and debentures), and equity securities; e.g., common stocks. The company or other entity issuing the _____ is called the issuer.

Chapter 22. International Business Finance

a. Book entry
b. Tracking stock
c. Securities lending
d. Security

27. _____ refers to the pricing of contributions (assets, tangible and intangible, services, and funds) transferred within an organization. For example, goods from the production division may be sold to the marketing division, or goods from a parent company may be sold to a foreign subsidiary. Since the prices are set within an organization (i.e. controlled), the typical market mechanisms that establish prices for such transactions between third parties may not apply.

a. Price index
b. Transfer pricing
c. Price discrimination
d. Discounts and allowances

28. A _____ is an international bond that is denominated in a currency not native to the country where it is issued. It can be categorised according to the currency in which it is issued. London is one of the centers of the _____ market, but _____s may be traded throughout the world - for example in Singapore or Tokyo.

a. Economic entity
b. Education production function
c. Interest rate option
d. Eurobond

29. _____s are deposits denominated in United States dollars at banks outside the United States, and thus are not under the jurisdiction of the Federal Reserve. Consequently, such deposits are subject to much less regulation than similar deposits within the United States, allowing for higher margins. There is nothing 'European' about _____ deposits; a US dollar-denominated deposit in Tokyo or Caracas would likewise be deemed _____ deposits.

a. AAB
b. Eurodollar
c. ABN Amro
d. A Random Walk Down Wall Street

30. _____ is a type of risk faced by investors, corporations, and governments. It is a risk that can be understood and managed with proper aforethought and investment.

Broadly, _____ refers to the complications businesses and governments may face as a result of what are commonly referred to as political decisions--or 'any political change that alters the expected outcome and value of a given economic action by changing the probability of achieving business objectives.' .

a. Mid price
b. Single-index model
c. Capital asset
d. Political risk

ANSWER KEY

Chapter 1

1. d	2. c	3. d	4. a	5. d	6. d	7. d	8. d	9. d	10. c
11. d	12. c	13. a	14. c	15. d	16. c	17. d	18. d	19. d	20. d
21. d	22. d	23. c	24. a	25. d	26. b	27. a	28. c	29. d	30. d
31. d	32. d	33. d	34. a	35. d	36. d	37. d	38. a	39. c	40. b
41. b	42. d	43. a	44. a	45. d	46. b	47. c	48. d	49. d	50. a
51. d	52. a								

Chapter 2

1. a	2. c	3. a	4. d	5. d	6. d	7. b	8. c	9. d	10. b
11. c	12. c	13. d	14. d	15. a	16. d	17. c	18. d	19. b	20. d
21. d	22. a	23. a	24. a	25. d	26. b	27. b	28. b	29. b	30. d
31. c	32. d	33. d	34. a	35. d	36. d	37. b	38. d	39. d	40. b
41. c	42. b	43. d	44. d	45. a	46. d	47. b	48. d	49. d	

Chapter 3

1. b	2. b	3. a	4. d	5. b	6. c	7. d	8. d	9. b	10. d
11. b	12. d	13. d	14. b	15. d	16. d	17. c	18. a	19. d	20. d
21. a	22. d	23. d	24. d	25. d	26. d	27. a	28. c	29. d	

Chapter 4

1. d	2. a	3. b	4. d	5. a	6. c	7. d	8. b	9. d	10. d
11. d	12. d	13. d	14. a	15. d	16. b	17. c	18. d	19. d	20. d

Chapter 5

1. c	2. c	3. d	4. d	5. b	6. c	7. b	8. d	9. d	10. c
11. b	12. d	13. b	14. b	15. a	16. b	17. c	18. d	19. d	

Chapter 6

1. b	2. c	3. d	4. b	5. d	6. d	7. d	8. a	9. c	10. d
11. d	12. d	13. d	14. d	15. d	16. c	17. a	18. b	19. d	20. d
21. a	22. d	23. b	24. b	25. d	26. d	27. d	28. d	29. b	30. d
31. a	32. d	33. a	34. a	35. d					

Chapter 7

1. b	2. d	3. d	4. d	5. d	6. d	7. b	8. a	9. d	10. a
11. d	12. d	13. b	14. a	15. d	16. b	17. a	18. d	19. d	20. d
21. d	22. d	23. a	24. c	25. d	26. d	27. c	28. b	29. d	30. d
31. a	32. b	33. b	34. d	35. d					

Chapter 8

1. b	2. d	3. d	4. b	5. b	6. c	7. d	8. d	9. d	10. d
11. b	12. a	13. a	14. d	15. d	16. d	17. d	18. d	19. d	20. b
21. d	22. d	23. b	24. b	25. d	26. c	27. c	28. d		

Chapter 9
1. c   2. d   3. d   4. a   5. b   6. b   7. d   8. b   9. a   10. d
11. d   12. b

Chapter 10
1. d   2. d   3. a   4. a   5. d   6. c   7. b   8. d   9. a   10. d
11. b   12. d   13. d   14. c   15. c   16. c   17. d   18. d   19. a   20. c
21. c   22. a   23. d   24. c   25. c

Chapter 11
1. b   2. d   3. a   4. d   5. d   6. d   7. a   8. a   9. b   10. a
11. d   12. d   13. c   14. c   15. d   16. d   17. a

Chapter 12
1. d   2. a   3. b   4. d   5. a   6. b   7. d   8. c   9. a   10. d
11. d   12. d   13. d   14. d   15. d   16. c   17. b   18. d   19. d   20. c
21. b   22. d   23. d   24. b   25. d   26. d   27. d   28. d   29. d   30. b

Chapter 13
1. d   2. d   3. d   4. d   5. d   6. b   7. d   8. d   9. d   10. b
11. d   12. d   13. d   14. c   15. b   16. d   17. a   18. b   19. d   20. b
21. d   22. d   23. a

Chapter 14
1. b   2. a   3. a   4. c   5. d   6. d   7. b   8. d   9. d   10. c
11. d   12. d   13. d   14. b   15. b   16. b   17. d   18. d   19. d   20. d
21. d   22. d   23. b   24. c   25. d   26. a   27. a   28. d   29. d   30. a
31. d   32. b   33. d   34. d   35. b   36. c   37. d   38. d   39. d   40. d
41. b   42. d   43. b   44. d   45. d   46. d   47. d   48. d   49. d

Chapter 15
1. d   2. d   3. c   4. d   5. a   6. c   7. a   8. d   9. c   10. d
11. d   12. b   13. c   14. a   15. c   16. b   17. d   18. d   19. d

Chapter 16
1. b   2. c   3. d   4. c   5. d   6. c   7. d   8. d   9. c   10. c
11. d   12. d   13. d   14. d   15. b   16. b   17. b   18. a   19. d   20. d
21. d   22. b   23. d   24. a   25. d   26. d   27. b   28. d   29. d   30. a
31. d   32. a   33. d   34. b   35. c   36. d   37. a   38. b   39. c   40. d
41. b   42. a   43. c

ANSWER KEY

Chapter 17
1. a	2. c	3. d	4. a	5. b	6. c	7. c	8. d	9. a	10. b
11. d	12. d	13. a	14. c	15. d	16. a	17. c	18. c	19. d	20. a
21. d	22. d	23. d	24. c	25. d	26. c				

Chapter 18
1. d	2. a	3. d	4. d	5. d	6. b	7. a	8. d	9. d	10. d
11. b	12. b	13. c	14. d	15. d	16. a	17. d	18. a	19. a	20. a
21. d	22. d	23. b	24. a	25. d	26. d	27. c	28. b	29. d	30. a
31. b	32. c	33. b	34. c	35. d	36. d	37. a	38. d	39. d	

Chapter 19
1. c	2. d	3. c	4. d	5. d	6. b	7. b	8. c	9. d	10. a
11. a	12. d	13. d	14. d	15. a	16. b	17. d	18. b	19. c	20. c
21. d	22. d	23. c	24. a	25. d	26. b	27. d	28. d	29. d	30. d

Chapter 20
1. c	2. d	3. d	4. b	5. d	6. a	7. b	8. d	9. a	10. c
11. d	12. b	13. a	14. c						

Chapter 21
1. d	2. c	3. c	4. b	5. b	6. d	7. c	8. a	9. d	10. d
11. d	12. d	13. d	14. d	15. d	16. a	17. d	18. d	19. c	20. d
21. b	22. b	23. b	24. b	25. d	26. d	27. d	28. d	29. d	30. b
31. c	32. b	33. b	34. a	35. a	36. d	37. c	38. b	39. d	40. d
41. c	42. d	43. a	44. b	45. d	46. d				

Chapter 22
1. d	2. a	3. b	4. d	5. b	6. b	7. d	8. d	9. d	10. d
11. b	12. d	13. b	14. d	15. d	16. d	17. d	18. a	19. c	20. a
21. d	22. b	23. b	24. b	25. a	26. d	27. b	28. d	29. b	30. d

www.ingramcontent.com/pod-product-compliance
Lightning Source LLC
Chambersburg PA
CBHW082205230426
43672CB00015B/2904